essential home

essential home

RYLAND
PETERS
& SMALL
LONDON NEW YORK

Judith Wilson

photography by JAN BALDWIN

Designer Catherine Randy
Commissioning editor Annabel Morgan
Location research manager Kate Brunt
Production Patricia Harrington
Art director Gabriella Le Grazie
Publishing director Alison Starling

Stylist Judith Wilson

First published in the USA in 2002
by Ryland Peters & Small, Inc.
519 Broadway
5th Floor
New York, NY 10012
www.rylandpeters.com

10 9 8 7 6 5 4 3 2

ISBN 1 84172 307 X

Library of Congress Cataloging-in-Publication Data

Wilson, Judith, 1962-
    Essential Home : putting together your perfect home /
by Judith Wilson.
        p. cm
    Includes index.
    ISBN 1-84172-307-X
    1. Interior decoration. I. Title.

  NK2115 . W8153 2002
  747--dc21

Printed and bound in China

Front cover: Didier Gomez's apartment in Paris

contents

6   introduction

8   *defining components*
10 making real lists and wish lists
14 classics
20 basics
26 luxuries
32 dressing up

38 *basic and luxury rooms*
40 living rooms
62 eating rooms
80 kitchens
98 bedrooms
120 bathrooms

138 suppliers
140 picture credits
142 index
144 acknowledgements

introduction

We can all use a little help when putting together our homes. Frequently, it is the initial planning of rooms—selecting wall colors, the choice of flooring underfoot—which is the easy part. Far harder are the decisions that arise after the paint cans have been put away. What should go into each room? Which items will endure, give most pleasure? What's the most hard-working combination of furniture? It's a myth that good-looking rooms naturally emerge just by putting back all your favorite things.

Key items, from chairs to ceramics, need careful planning if a chosen look is to last. Get these choices right, and you'll be equipped with the decorative building blocks for a flexible home, one that evolves with fashion and your own changing tastes. Stick too rigidly to one style, be too swayed by current trends, and you'll be stuck in a decorative timewarp and regret impulse buys. There is no blueprint for the contents of the perfect home, but this book will help you devise your own unique formula. Far from taking the fun out of decorating, time invested now will provide you with a foundation upon which to build, reducing the risk factor of future purchases and giving you freedom to experiment with fashion and contemporary buys.

If overhauling the contents of your entire home seems daunting, divide up its components. Think, for a moment, of fashion, and those categories most of us subconsciously use to compose any outfit, simple or elaborate. Every wardrobe contains classic pieces—the chic black suit, the pair of jeans—which form the backbone to any given look. Then there are the basics, from plain white T-shirts to gray socks, and the luxuries, from a scarlet cashmere sweater to a silk shirt. Finally, there are the accessories, the more individual and eclectic the better. As a formula, what matters is that this provides an unbeatable framework for getting started: after that, it can be interpreted in myriad different styles.

So take those same principles and try them at home. Start by considering your furniture as the classic pieces. Think of the hard-working staples, such as towels, cups, and glasses, as your basics, and the pretty pieces—a velvet pillow or mohair throw—as your luxuries. Then, last but not least, there are the accessories, from paintings to vases: that crucial, final "dressing up" stage. Does it sound foolproof? It should, because it is. Follow these simple guidelines, and your essential home will emerge—one that's flexible, fashionable, and guaranteed to last.

defining components

making real lists and wish lists

Just as any successful wardrobe is the result of careful shopping and constant re-editing, so too the existing contents of your home need proper attention before it will work efficiently. Whether you choose to reassess just before moving home, or at any stage, this is essentially a practical process. You need to allot time for making lists of what you already own, what you want to lose, and what you plan to acquire. It shouldn't be an overwhelming task. Make it fun—think of what you're doing as a creative inventory. Equip yourself with a beautiful notebook or a large box file, specially designated for the job, and do your thinking over weeks, even months, to allow plenty of time for reflection and planning.

First, reacquaint yourself with what you have at home. Walk around each room, opening all the cabinets and drawers, and noting down what you find, putting objects into categories, from classics to accessories. Underscore the things you love and that work well; asterisk those that are rarely used. Next, take a mental trawl around each room and ask yourself what you really need to own, and what you'd love to possess. Compare all your lists. Which items should go? What should replace them? What should stay? Be honest. If you've given house room to an inherited sofa that jars stylistically, then summon the courage to offload it and save up for a classic design. If chunky glasses double as wine glasses, and that suits your style,

Left The simpler you want a room to look, the more editing is required, because the eye will be drawn straight to what is left in the room. Make a point of removing extraneous items while making your lists and decisions. It is a remarkably useful discipline to strip a room back down to basics—a new beauty will emerge from even the plainest arrangement of its contents. Here, fresh white bed linen plus a single picture create a remarkably tranquil bedroom.

Above right Larger items of furniture, such as sofas, beds, tables, and dining chairs, represent big investment buys that you won't want to replace in a hurry. You will need to prioritize which pieces should go on a real list, to buy now, and which items can go on your wish list, to be purchased and introduced over a longer time scale.

Right When you are compiling your lists, don't forget to group smaller decorative items into individual categories. Vases are one example. List them in terms of shape, size, and color to provide as much variety of choice as possible.

then allot your budget to items that you do need. List-making will focus the mind and helps you make informed decisions.

Your real lists will be composed of all the items that are either used daily at home (plates, a table), or that have a very specific function (the toaster, the bed pillows). They won't all be basics; furniture and decorative items will feature as well. Be aware that most items will be things you need only one, or one set of, to keep your home running with minimum fuss. Even if, practically speaking, you think you have everything you need, take another look. Does everything look good and mix well with other items? This is the perfect opportunity to weed out those flowery saucepans and colored towels that irk you, and replace them with simple, classic designs that go with everything.

By contrast, on your wish lists will be the more decorative items, those that add visual flair and give you a decorative choice. These are the interiors equivalent of "me time." Whether your personal wish list includes a dozen lime-green linen napkins or a sparkling chandelier, what

counts is that the objects fit into your budget and time scale. Don't feel guilty about buying lovely things for your home. And if you do, there's nothing quite like putting your wishes in writing to validate the need for them! Wish lists can also help you prioritize. Instead of lusting after a velvet armchair, you might realize that a velvet footstool will satisfy your need, be less of a commitment, decoratively speaking, and cost less money.

Think about budget, and how much money you can allocate to your home. The whole point of a reassessment is *not* to tempt you to buy lots of new things; on the contrary, it is intended to save money long-term. Yet it's also nice to know that, having located the gaps, you can gradually begin to fill them. Plan to realize your lists over monthly, annual, or five-yearly time scales—whatever suits your finances. Knowing the available budget will affect your lists in other ways, too. In a sensible world, those items on the real lists should be bought first. Yet we all need frivolity, so if you're going to blow funds, at least do it on a planned and longed-for luxury.

Opposite page **Just as everyone's definition of a treat is different, every individual's wish list will vary wildly. One person may consider a Thirties pythonskin chair as the last word in decorative chic; another may prefer the up-to-minute looks of a satin- and faux-fur-backed throw. Choosing antique pieces, which can be passed down the generations, may be another priority. So when making the wish lists, don't just note down the pieces that immediately spring to mind. Try to expand your horizons and figure out new preferences. Take a few days out and treat yourself to some window shopping, perhaps with a friend who has a different style, so that there are other opinions on offer. Investigate chain stores and boutiques, antique and contemporary pieces, small craft workshops, and secondhand stores to get a full range of choices.** *Above* **The best wish lists include a mix of objects, large and small, functional and decorative. Include a variety of price tags, so a small luxury, such as a scented candle, is immediately affordable.**

Left Many people buy, or hang on to, a piece of furniture just because it goes with everything. That's fine, but add to those criteria the fact that it should be able to stand alone and still look good. However simple the piece, the silhouette and materials must be pleasing. At home, look at a piece you can't decide about in isolation; in a store, ask to have the sofa you're deciding on moved away from other models.

classics

In the same way that a wardrobe classic withstands seasons and trends—think of the trench coat, the jeans jacket—so too the larger, most fundamental pieces of furniture you pick need to endure. Furniture is invariably an investment, so it pays to choose well. A good piece, of classic design, should last many decades, both practically, without sagging stuffing or peeling veneers, and visually, adapting to changing trends around it. Take your time when choosing; buy the best you can afford; and be sure the furniture is practical, comfortable, and user-friendly as well as good to look at.

Before buying anything new, refer to your lists and see what you already have to play with. Take Polaroid pictures or snapshots of each piece and stick them in your notebook, devoting one page to each room. Viewing your furniture out of context will help highlight what shapes and styles you already have and what the gaps are. Draw a scale plan of each room, and work out how much floor space the existing furniture occupies and whether there's room for anything else. You'll also know, from making the lists, if there are specific pieces of furniture your home is lacking.

Look through the pictures of your furniture with a critical eye, and be ruthless. If there is a piece that is ugly or uncomfortable, get rid of it. It's far better to do without a coffee table until you can afford the right one, than let a fussy piece upset the balance of an entire room. If a piece of furniture doesn't work simply because it is the wrong color, or has unattractive or dated upholstery, consider whether repainting or re-upholstering will make a difference. It's amazing how

Opposite page, below left If you've opted for a contemporary shape but are worried a piece will go out of fashion too quickly, then choosing neutral upholstery, rather than a trendy pattern or color, can play a significant role in taking the edge off modernity.

This page Not every piece of furniture has to fulfill a functional role. When reassessing the contents of your home, see if there are empty areas—a hall, corner of a room, or landing—that could be given more character by installing a pretty and unique piece. Look for furniture finishes that improve with age—leather, plaster molding, gilding, "foxed" mirrors, and antique wood are all good choices.

This page Decisions to buy, or keep, a major investment piece should be based not just on looks and durability, but on comfort, too. There are no long-term benefits to be had from a dynamically styled retro sofa if it is too short to lounge on (if that's your preference) or doesn't have enough suspension to make sitting pleasurable. Don't be afraid to bounce on beds, curl up on chairs, and sit at a potential dining table when visiting furniture showrooms, and make sure your partner does so, too!

Right Before discarding them as old-fashioned, sift through inherited antique pieces and visualize them mixed with your contemporary furnishings. Most rooms will benefit from the inclusion of at least one period piece, as the more fluid lines and aged materials lend individuality.

an out-moded sofa, for example, can "disappear" in a room once it is re-covered in a neutral fabric. Don't get rid of something just because it has slipped out of fashion. Put it in storage, or lend it out. The current vogue for retro furniture proves that most trends come around again.

If, once your reassessment is complete, you are planning to buy new furniture, think carefully about how it will fit with existing pieces. Don't buy a very modern sofa on the assumption that, one day, you'll change everything else to match it. Few of us have the budget to be so radical. It is reassuring to realize that the most appealing mix of furniture has always been a combination of different periods and shapes. This mix is the most forgiving in terms of changing trends, because you can add and take away one or two trendy pieces of furniture while other, more classic pieces remain as the timeless framework of the room.

So how can you be sure, when you buy, that a design will still please and feel "right" in twenty years' time? One failsafe method is to opt for some antique pieces in a traditional style that has weathered centuries, let alone decades. Of course fashions wax and wane, even among antiques, but you can't go far wrong with the simple lines and attractive woods of classics such as a nineteenth-century French country cabriole-legged dining table, a Shaker chest, or a Chesterfield sofa. Provided they are simply styled, and mixed with contemporary pieces, they will hold their appeal. Twentieth-century designs by modern greats such as Le Corbusier and Arne Jacobsen have also earned status as classics. And if the rising cost of the real thing is too much, then there are excellent re-editions on the market.

Above and top right Like the basic white plate, which can be mixed with any style, simple or sophisticated, there are certain failsafe furniture choices that will go with anything. The white or pale neutral sofa or armchair is one of them. Pick a slipcover in a washable, preshrunk fabric such as cotton or linen-cotton mix, so that practicality is assured. Then enjoy the flexibility it affords. One year it can be dressed up with a high-fashion silver sequinned cushion; a couple of years later moved to a bedroom with faded chintz curtains, and later still be teamed with a leather-trimmed throw and added to a more grown-up living room.

Above right If it's proving hard to work out your own definition of a classic furniture buy, look first at the accessories you know to be classics—those, such as a lamp, which combine great design with practicality—then apply the same criteria to furniture.

Opposite page Furniture can be adapted. If an armoire looks great, but the hanging space is cramped, customize the interior with shelves for folded clothes, and find somewhere else to hang dresses.

Secondhand stores and auctions are another good source of simpler classics. Old school desks, a marble-topped kitchen table, a church pew, or an office map chest are all possible options. Not only will these pieces be cheaper than true antiques, but also—because they are less precious—you will have more freedom to alter or update them if you wish. A dilapidated overmantel mirror could be repainted with a wash of Swedish blue, or a humble trestle table topped with stainless steel for a more contemporary look. In five years' time, the colors and finishes can be changed again if you wish.

The panic can really set in when you have committed to buying a new piece of furniture, and a contemporary style at that. Interior fashions seem to come and go with alarming speed, and it's worrying to think that a couch bought now might soon be out of date. But furniture trends don't alter as quickly as you might think. Do your research, and try to identify any particularly strong trends among cutting-edge furniture designers, just as the chain stores start to produce less expensive copies. That way, you'll get maximum style mileage for your money. Your choice will also be dependent on your budget. If you adore a defining piece by an acclaimed contemporary furniture designer, and can afford it, then you are probably assured of a classic that will endure for your lifetime. If funds are limited, opt for the chain-store option. And if you want a fashionable look without the investment, buy cheap, trendy, smaller items like stools or side tables that won't induce guilt when you cast them aside in a few years' time.

As with your classic wardrobe staples, major pieces of furniture should be in neutral colors or materials, so they can withstand changing fashions in color and pattern. Upholstery can range from white through to cream, biscuit, gray, and black; neutral leather and suede will also stand the test of time. Although it might seem that any type of wood goes with anything, be aware that there are vogues for different wood finishes, too. Steer clear of current overly trendy varieties, such as wenge, and try instead to pick a wood that genuinely pleases your eye. Other natural fibers and materials that work well with most things include wicker, glass, and leather, all of which also weather beautifully over time.

As with classic wardrobe staples, your major pieces of furniture should be in neutral colors and materials, so they can withstand changing fashions in color and pattern.

This page **Fabric furnishings—from slipcovers to curtains and shades—are often treated as "fixed" elements that can't be changed once they've been coordinated in terms of color or pattern to the decoration. Yet there's a more flexible alternative. By thinking of them as items to be added to, or mixed and matched with other pieces, you have an altogether more fluid formula. So choose slipcovers in place of upholstery, and unlined tie-on or clip-on curtains, which can be swapped for other drapes when the mood takes you. White or neutrals always make the most adaptable choices.**

Opposite page, above **One of the main advantages of amassing simple, pure designs is that they won't go out of date, yet when mixed with a splash of something trendy can also look supremely modern. So, for flexibility, always look for plain unadorned versions of your everyday basics.**

Opposite page, below **Basics can be cheap, but they don't have to be. If the budget is there, you can seek out the best-quality, most refined materials, from porcelain plates to neutral linen pillow covers.**

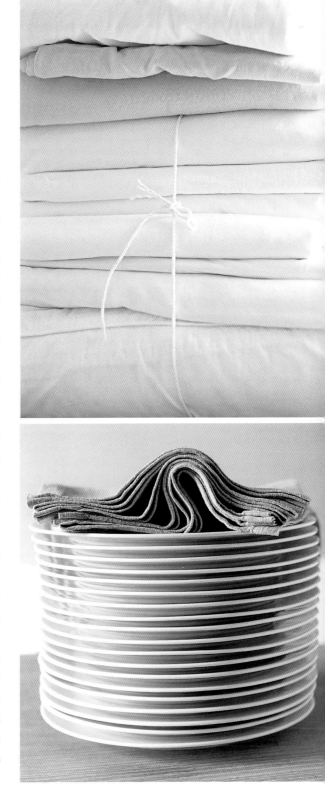

basics

Basics are those hard-working household items that you use daily, and which constitute the broad fabric of any home's contents. They range from hardware (pillows, pillow forms) and the purely functional (a toaster, a clock) through to a raft of everyday necessities, from dishes and sheets to towels and candlesticks. It helps to include some decorative items—vases and mirrors, photo frames and lamps—within this category, too. No home, however simple, is complete without a well-edited collection of simple accessories.

Chosen with care, basics are the things that help your home run like clockwork and look good on a day-to-day basis, so you need to give them barely a second thought (or glance). Humble as many of them seem, it pays to select them carefully. A great basic—let's say, a sturdy, beautifully shaped plain glass pitcher—can, and should, give pleasure and service for a lifetime. Just as any architect will tell you that focusing attention on the little things—a door handle or shade pull—can give great sensual, visual, and practical pleasure, re-evaluating your basics will do the same. We all need a toilet brush and a laundry basket, so why not pick an appealing design?

Basics need to be supremely practical since they are used daily. You will know, from your lists, the items that have worked well and lasted over the years, and those that haven't. Learn from experience. It may be something very simple, like acknowledging that cheap cotton dishtowels shrink and that the investment in traditional linen ones really is worthwhile. Think and question before you buy. Will those inexpensive wine glasses withstand the dishwasher? Will foam-filled pillow forms flatten too soon? Does a great-looking white teapot actually pour efficiently? When shopping for specialized wares, such as kitchen goods or bed linen, look carefully at what commercial enterprises use. There's a reason why restaurants use stainless-steel cookware, and top hotels choose pure linen sheets. It's because they are practical, and they last.

Just as simple designs—the short-sleeved T-shirt, the plain leather belt—are the basic components of a successful wardrobe, so clean lines and pared-down shapes make sensible home basics. This has a practical bonus. If one part of a set gets lost or broken, it's likely you'll find a replica or a similar replacement—even in five years' time—that fits in perfectly. Then there are the visual benefits. A truly classic design, such as a gooseneck lamp, a Duralex glass, or a wooden photo frame, will never go out of date. More importantly, plain and simple pieces will go with everything, can be dressed up or down, and will probably look just as appropriate in a kitchen as in a bedroom. The search for the perfectly designed basic isn't always as easy as it might seem, however. It's amazing how many items you will need to disregard—because of fussy, unnecessary detailing—before you can find the requisite simplicity. Enjoy that hunt—it will be worth it.

You needn't restrict yourself entirely to classic designs. For years, fashion designers have reinterpreted traditional garments such as the white shirt, inventing modern, quirky, or plain eccentric variations. You only have to look in the chain stores, or at pieces by contemporary designers, to see that the same is true of homewares. So have some fun. Why shouldn't a plain glass wine carafe sport a hole in the middle? By all means go for white plates, but instead of standard glaze, look for flat finishes, or choose a square silhouette instead of round. Opt for practical white window shades, but pick the design featuring punched holes as a quirky twist.

Below, left and right **Another great way to compile your personal set of basics is to think through a typical twenty-four hours at home. What do you use, sit on, eat from, and look in (or at) on a daily basis? Making a list this way will help to deflect thinking from just the small things (tableware, towels) and focus attention on larger essentials such as a full-length mirror or coffee table. The point about basics, too, is that they should always be in natural, sturdy materials that will mix with a variety of styles.**

This page **Playing down window treatments to the absolute minimum is a failsafe way to create a blank canvas against which furniture and decorative items can shine. Few people can cope without any screen at the window, but good plain options include unlined linen panels, attached to the frame itself, a roll-up or plain Roman shade, wood Venetian blinds, or plantation shutters. Pick your choice in neutral tones, then there will still be the opportunity to add more elaborate window dressings at a later date.**

In terms of color, it does make sense to stick to a neutral palette for the majority of your household basics. That doesn't mean that absolutely everything has to be white or beige. You can also include shades of cream and biscuit, black and gray in all its tones, even navy. Natural fibers and materials are also excellent choices. Think of metal (galvanized vases, contemporary lamps), wood (from platters to candlesticks), wicker (baskets and placemats), and leather (from footstools to storage boxes). Visually, neutral basics provide the optimum blank canvas. Once that is in place, you are much freer to experiment with new colors and unusual textures when adding in your luxuries and accessories. That said, if you spot a great basic in a wonderful color, snap it up. A jewel-colored glass vase to mix with plain ones, or a primary-colored rubber bathmat make everyday living so much more fun.

Think about budget and quality, too. Amassing a good range of plain basics isn't simply about seeking out the cheapest and most utilitarian items. A simple basic may be cheap or expensive, made from plain cotton or pure linen; but what matters is that it looks good in its own right, mixes happily with plenty of accessories, and performs its function well. So, you should tailor your choices to your budget. A set of plain white dinner plates could be from a wholesale store, or could be exquisite white porcelain of the finest quality. An occasional wooden side table can be a chain-store bargain, or a retro furniture investment. Sticking to simplicity means that when you do have the funds, you can make a seamless shift from cheap wine glasses to crystal, from cotton sheets to linen.

And remember that once you have all your plain basics in place, you can enjoy them on two completely different levels. A simple wooden dining table, covered with a white tablecloth, set with plain glassware and white china, and surrounded with a set of classic ladder-backed chairs, works admirably well for everyday living. But put those same components together with just a couple of luxury items—a vivid silk table runner, perhaps, and a set of hand-blown jewel-colored wine glasses—and that very same dining room will enter a totally new dimension.

A simple basic may be cheap or expensive, made from plain cotton or pure linen; but what matters is that it looks good in its own right.

Opposite page, above Once the concept of basics is understood, it's a personal choice whether you choose utility styles or more sophisticated incarnations. The current vogue for industrial chic is particularly appropriate in lofts, city apartments, or modern country homes. In terms of furniture, search for reclaimed factory or school furniture, from metal and canvas chairs to wooden lunchroom tables. Smaller accessories might include cafeteria-style glass plates and cups, or striped cotton cafeteria-towels.

Opposite page, below Take time to search for the perfect white mug or correctly weighted stainless-steel flatware. If looks and functionality matter to you, it's worth getting it right with the things that meet your eye and pass through your hands each and every day.
This page Make practicality as much a priority as good looks. Screw-on lids really must be airtight, and a towel must absorb water well. In addition to checking out reliable suppliers, ask friends if there are certain products they have owned that have lasted well.

This page Any "fixed" features—from a padded headboard to an upholstered stool—are best in a neutral shade. This gives flexibility: fashionable colors can easily be added, while tone-on-tone neutrals will create a sophisticated look. Light-colored fabrics such as suede or velvet can be difficult to keep pristine. Go for darker neutrals—eggplant or mushroom—or choose a more practical material, such as leather.

luxuries

Everyone deserves a little luxury, and so does every home. In recent years, influenced by trends in both fashion and interiors, we've gradually embraced the idea that it's okay to treat ourselves. We've also been exposed to the more obvious signs of luxury: slippery satins and opulent velvets, exquisite detailing from embroidery to sequins. If you want to create a full-blown boudoir-style bedroom, for example, then all the components, from silk sheets to mirrored dressers, are available in stores. But should you prefer the more modest concept of a few fine luxuries to be mixed in with a simple, tailored interior, that's possible too. It doesn't matter if your beautiful things are rarely in daily use and

only come out of storage occasionally. What counts is that they will add visual bite, sensory pleasure, and individuality to a room.

By definition, a luxury is something you love, so during your home appraisal, you're more likely to be making wish lists of lovely things you long for, rather than ousting items that no longer fit in. Be realistic about your budget. If you have limited funds, remember that you can plan and save up for a longed-for item. Some luxuries are very affordable. The addition of scented incense sticks or mother-of-pearl salt pots to a simple table setting will look good and make you feel pampered. Tailor your luxury to what suits your current lifestyle, too. Far better to forgo the cream

Above left Layers of detail, concentrated on a single outrageous piece in a room, can be as effective as several glamorous items dotted around. Beautiful pillows are the perfect vehicle for creating such a layered effect. Try contrast backings, mixing mat and shiny fabrics, silk or fur, embroidery or beading, or go for a solid fabric edged with something exotic such as feathers or a ruched satin border. *Above right* Sometimes, the whole point about a luxury purchase is that it is utterly without function, but simply looks gorgeous. Think not just in terms of texture and color, but of sinuous shapes and a great silhouette.

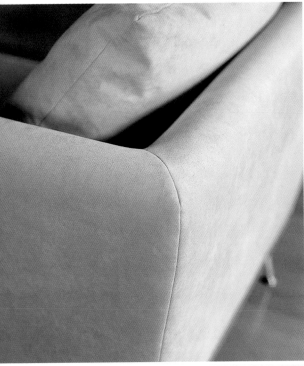

Concentrate on items made from high-quality materials with great workmanship. Like a designer purse, these things don't come cheap, but they will last a lifetime.

cashmere blankets if you have children, and opt instead for a crystal-beaded tablecloth to be used for grown-up dinner parties only. Think of practicality. If a silk eiderdown has to be constantly dry-cleaned, ask yourself whether that really is a luxury, or an expensive mistake?

Luxury is also an entirely subjective notion, so before you buy anything, it's essential to crystallize your own definition. Some of us will take it at face value, and go all out for tactile or visual splendor in direct contrast to plain and simple basics. But there's no point in buying a dozen dramatic gold charger plates, if your true vision of luxury is a top-of-the-line stainless-steel juicer that really works. If you're struggling to define your personal vision, think about the luxuries you have in your own fashion wardrobe. Do you prefer to add a single panné velvet scarf to a sharply tailored suit; or layer a silk shirt over a chiffon skirt, then add a variety of accessories? Whatever your style, it's likely you will feel comfortable with a similar combination in the home.

For those with a naturally pared-down style, it makes sense to concentrate on items made from high-quality materials with great workmanship. Like a designer purse, these things don't come cheap, but they will last a lifetime, and the design is likely to be a classic. Into this category fall sets of linen or Egyptian cotton sheets, silver rather than silver-plated flatware, or a tooled leather chair. Even if visitors don't notice the difference, you will enjoy the subtle quality in the look and feel of each item. Think not just of accessories, but more laterally. Perhaps you want to re-upholster a headboard in heavy linen, instead of denim, or replace a budget set of polypropylene chairs in similar materials but with cutting-edge designer styling? Your luxury might simply be to invest in a duck-down comforter and pillows for the best night's sleep ever.

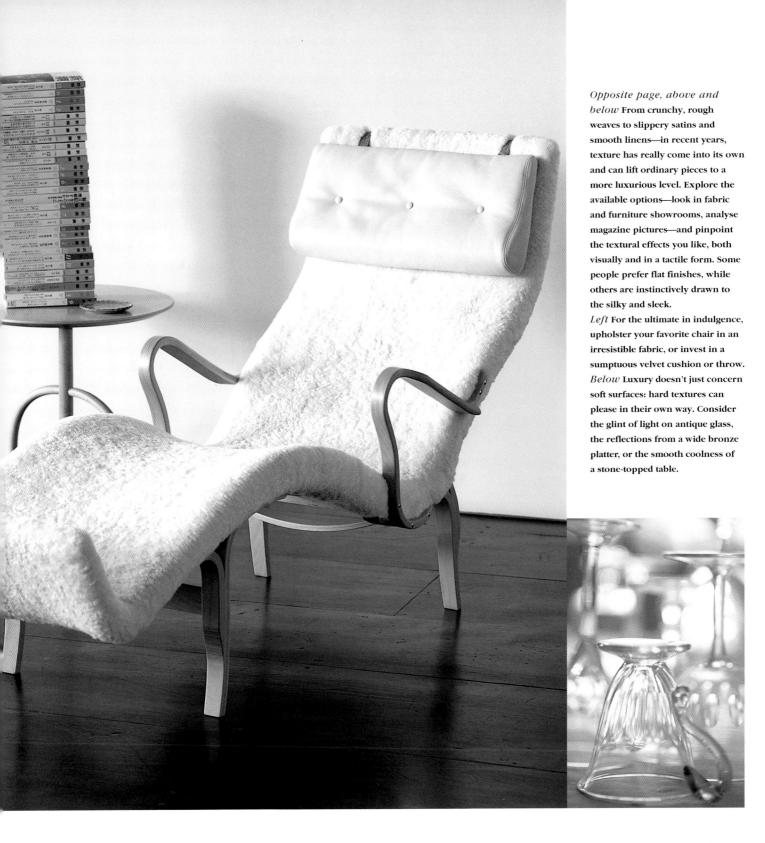

Opposite page, above and below From crunchy, rough weaves to slippery satins and smooth linens—in recent years, texture has really come into its own and can lift ordinary pieces to a more luxurious level. Explore the available options—look in fabric and furniture showrooms, analyse magazine pictures—and pinpoint the textural effects you like, both visually and in a tactile form. Some people prefer flat finishes, while others are instinctively drawn to the silky and sleek.

Left For the ultimate in indulgence, upholster your favorite chair in an irresistible fabric, or invest in a sumptuous velvet cushion or throw.

Below Luxury doesn't just concern soft surfaces: hard textures can please in their own way. Consider the glint of light on antique glass, the reflections from a wide bronze platter, or the smooth coolness of a stone-topped table.

When investing in a luxury item, which is expensive, it can be hard to justify the cost—after all, you don't really *need* those hand-painted silk lampshades. But if you are convinced you will appreciate such an item every time you see it, then save up, make the investment, and enjoy it without guilt. Owning luxuries is about treating yourself to a bit of fun and frivolity at home. It's also worth asking yourself whether it's essential to stick to neutral colors. If you adore bright shades, and it's a choice between bright-pink silk and muted gray, trust your instincts and go for the color that most lifts your spirits. Far better to do this than buy something in a particular color just because it happens to be fashionable this season.

Think about the notion of luxury, too, in terms of made-to-order items at home. While, in fashion, haute couture is for the minority, many men get suits made to measure for not much more than an off-the-rail price. So consider having items made to your own specification. Many sofa manufacturers and furniture stores will make pieces to longer dimensions for a small extra cost,

and if you entertain frequently, owning a large dining table that sits twelve comfortably may be the only luxury you crave. If you are fussy about finding particular patterns or specific colors, then commissioning a custommade rug or specially dyed fabric might be your idea of heaven.

When it comes to mixing luxury items with everything else at home, remember that a little splash of something beautiful goes a long way. Provided you have created a classic, neutral backdrop, you will need only one scarlet silk throw pillow to create impact; just one set of jeweled napkin rings on a plain table, not a gilded set of china. Once you start to experiment with the mix, it will become obvious why luxury items should be added in, rather than fixed components. In a pared-down bedroom, for example, you might want to create a more seductive mood. Do so with a satin-upholstered headboard, and you are stuck with the look until you can re-upholster. But hang silk curtains over plain white blinds, and you have the option to return the room to neutrality when that particular fashion has passed.

Opposite page **Anyone who has watched a child nestling into a soft blanket will know how sensuous different textures are. Yet, as adults, we often lose our connection with that highly developed tactile sense. Try to retrieve it. Don't automatically think that luxury equals rich velvet, ribbed chenille, faux fur, and pure wool. Cotton variations, from loose-knit cellular blankets to padded cotton-covered throws and plump chintz-covered eiderdowns can be every bit as snug and inviting.**
Above, from left to right **Visual variety constitutes a treat just as much as precious materials. Whether picking tableware, ornaments or furniture, keep an eye out for off-beat colors, a wobbly, unexpected silhouette, or textures you want to touch. You need a handful of pieces guaranteed to pack a punch against the neutral canvas of the rest of the room, table, or bed. Don't underestimate the sensual power of a quality scented candle, incense stick, or oil. Good classic smells include fig, lilac, tuberose, cedar, and orange.**

Opposite page and left Often the most distinctive finishing touches are the most unexpected ones, so experiment by mixing contrasting styles and textures together. It may be obvious to team a white T-shirt with combat pants, but much more fun (and daring) to wear them with a gold crochet bikini top. Here, the same principles are applied to a basic kitchen, so the gilded flashes of mosaic lend instant exoticism to everyday odds and ends.

Right Every home needs "dress up" elements, specific to each room. It's fine to go for over-the-top buys, from gilded glassware to beaded napkins or lampshades, and even more fun when you find them cheaply in the outlet mall. The point is that they will be teamed with a neutral, plain backdrop, so will not overpower, just add spice. If you lack confidence, borrow outrageous accessories first from friends, to get an idea of which styles look best in your own home.

dressing up

Though the current vogue for minimalist interiors might make us think otherwise, accessories, paintings, and decorative detail are what stamp a room with interest and individuality. Interiors up and down the country may contain similar furniture, bought from chain stores, but no two rooms will ever look identical. In the same way that it's possible to personalize a simple outfit by adding unusual jewelry, bags, or hats, we all dress up our rooms in radically different ways. Selecting and arranging accessories is the fun part of creating an interior. Knowing that you have created a carefully balanced, neutral canvas of a room to build on gives you free rein to experiment with quirky, even wild, new looks that can be changed or toned down as years pass by.

Start first by taking a long hard look at the decorative pieces you already have. Most of us are ridiculously sentimental about certain ornaments, keeping them on display long after they've lost their appeal. Nothing ruins the look of a room, or dates it, more than unsuitable accessories. So be critical. It can be very helpful to go from room to room, gathering together all your odds and ends, plus paintings, and placing them in the middle of the room. This is an immensely useful activity to do on a regular basis, because it forces you to come up with new arrangements and imparts a new dynamic

Below, left and right The more eclectic the mix of decorative objects a room has on display, the more interesting it becomes as a space. Consciously combine things from different categories: a child's painting or papier-mâché model, a painting brought back from a favorite vacation destination, an ornament from your family's past, and "found" natural objects create a good basis. It's not so much the objects themselves that matter, but the out-of-context combinations that arise, and the clash of varying periods and materials.

Opposite page For those with a naturally pared-down, classic style, too many pieces will be anathema. Just remember that the fewer things there are on show, the more they will attract attention. Concentrate on creating a specific tableau—using a chair, a scaled-up pot or artefact, a bamboo ladder—but be prepared to keep changing it on a regular basis. If ornamentation is the lifeblood of a room, it's crucial to keep moving it on, so the look stays fresh and inspiring.

to the room. If you're dithering over an object, don't throw it away, store it. Many interiors decorators of the less-is-more discipline admit to constantly revolving accessories so each one gets an airing.

When your walls and surfaces are empty, this is the time to assess, in conjunction with your lists, what items you're looking for and where you should put them. Where are the obvious surfaces for display; where will sunlight naturally highlight an arrangement? Are there gaps not filled by furniture, where a painting could be propped? Does the color scheme seem too bland—do you need to introduce an exotic new texture or bright new shade? Scale is as important as the item itself when it comes to dressing up a room. Many people make the mistake of choosing lots of little ornaments when one huge mirror or bowl would create more impact.

Buying new accessories offers an opportunity to introduce fashion items that will instantly update a classic room. There's never been a better time to buy home accessories, and at brilliant prices; many of the chain stores have excelled themselves with beautiful copies of

designer-label looks. It's much easier to feel confident about splashing out on a funky Pucci-print scatter cushion or a satin lampshade when it's available at a budget price and you know you can replace it with something else in two years' time. If you have stuck carefully to a neutral scheme, now is the time to introduce the odd bright and fashionable piece of furniture.

Yet dressing up is as much about creating individuality as about keeping your interior up to date. So keep your eyes open in thrift stores and flea markets for anything eyecatching or unusual. The pieces you see and use needn't be designed as home ornaments. A child's pair of pink ballet slippers can look wonderful adorning a mantelpiece; an exquisite textile can be framed and hung on the wall. Papier-mâché artwork brought home from school will always withstand the test of time. One-off pieces from architectural reclamation yards are currently in vogue, and many decorators and antiques dealers display a salvaged piece—old iron stair-rods, or a work-room clock—as "art." Look out for one-off designs, too, while traveling abroad. Gold-embroidered silk table runners, hand-carved sculptures, and stone platters will all add up to an eclectic interior.

Dressing up a room successfully is also about how you display your objects. Look through magazines and in interiors books to see how stylists and designers arrange decorative finds. Experiment by mixing pieces from different periods or play with shapes and scales or clashing colors. If you want the "dressing up" to be subtle and restrained, restrict yourself to one or two bold but beautiful accessories, such as a giant platter or tall vase. When getting dressed, you would never put on all your pieces of jewelry at once; the principle is the same at home. And if there is an obvious area for display, such as a side table or mantelpiece, enjoy creating a little tableau. The fewer objects you show off, the more the emphasis will be placed upon them.

Accessories are generally the easiest things to change around in a room, and the most instant way to create a new look, so make sure your

decorative arrangements can be altered easily. Don't tie a room down with a rigid display of pictures, symmetrically anchored over a piece of furniture, or create a color scheme so dominant that cushion covers or lampshades can't be changed. Keep the ability to accessorize flexible. A mirror could be propped on a mantelpiece rather than hung; photos displayed in simple glass frames rather than mounted and hung on the wall. Use basic decorative items, such as plain glass vases, to make the usual look unusual. A deep container, filled with buttons, beads, shells, or old family letters will attract instant attention.

If you are a minimalist at heart, and don't like a cluttered look, you can still "dress up" a restrained room with subtle customizing. Think of fringing on the leading edge of a plain curtain, stud detailing on a neutral burlap-upholstered chair, or same-color embroidery or appliqué work on pillows. And when tastes swing around again to cluttered living, you will still have the ultimate blank canvas for adding a touch of exotic style.

If you are a minimalist at heart, and don't like a cluttered look, you can still "dress up" a restrained room with subtle customizing.

Opposite page, above and below Professional interior stylists quickly learn the art of making the ordinary look exotic or beautiful, so take a tip from them. Glass vases filled with balls of string or a shallow platter full of fruit create still lifes that are as visually stimulating as typical ornaments. *Opposite page, below left* Dressing up your home is the ultimate personal statement, so don't forget to put carefully chosen special objects on display. This heart-shaped stone, picked from the beach, has great symbolic value as well as looking beautiful.

This page Get brave with scale: either go very big or very small. Although the dimensions of the room will have some influence, ultimately it's the size and shape of the pieces you display that create the visual tricks. One giant canvas, propped against the wall, or a tiny painting, hung in isolation, will be much more exciting than a row of standard-sized canvases.

basic & luxury rooms

living rooms

The well-planned living room should be comfortable and tranquil, but above all a reflection of its owners' personality and tastes. The more restrained the shapes and colors of its major building blocks—sofas, chairs, tables—the more flexible a backdrop you will create for new pieces and accessories as fashions wax and wane.

living room basics

It's a common misconception that choosing a pretty fabric or a bold wall color will magically set a decorative seal on the living room. It won't. Look closely at photographs of any beautiful living room, and the bottom line is that if each piece is attractive in its own right, and cohesively arranged, surface decoration actually matters little. So when reassessing your room, make choosing good-looking, if simple, pieces the priority. And adopt a democratic mind-set. After all, this is a "public" room, where you'll entertain friends, so their comfort and pleasure matters almost as much as your own.

Your list-making process will have highlighted the essential pieces for any living room: a sofa, armchair, table, and bookshelf at the very least. But as you plan, ask even more pertinent questions and refine your list. If you entertain frequently, would two small sofas be better than one large couch? Might a daybed suit the room more than an armchair? And a coffee table isn't a necessity if small side tables will do the job just as well.

Think, too, about the practicality and quality of each piece you choose. Although the living room may be used only during evenings or at weekends, its major components need to last over a decade. So buy the best you can afford, and put your money into the most heavily used pieces. For example, the main sofa should have coil-sprung seats and duck-feather-filled cushions, but you could go for foam upholstery on an occasional

Opposite page This metropolitan living room proves that combining a very few carefully chosen pieces can still result in stylish good looks and a comfortable room. Here is the formula in a nutshell: classic, contemporary sofa, basic side tables, the luxury of an original artwork, and a quirky lamp and side table. *This page* A living room composed entirely of neutral tones, from gray upholstery fabric to pale woods and polished stone, provides the perfect blank canvas for unusual and eye-catching accessories. At a later date this room could be transformed by flamboyant and colorful accessories to provide an entirely new look.

This page and opposite When funds are limited and you are composing a living room from the true basics—couch, table, mirror, storage—keeping to neutral shades has an added bonus. Working with a mix of natural materials and with whites or creams makes it much easier to mix wildly differing styles, which may range from utility metal shelving *(opposite page, above right)* or a rustic wood table *(opposite page, below left)*, to quite ordinary, even distinctly unsexy chair or sofa shapes. Yet however different the types of furniture are, try to pick one or two that are—in your mind—the pivotal pieces in the room and that you are sure will remain over the years. The plain white sofa, battered leather armchairs, and two versions of a large mirror, as shown here, are good examples of such "key" pieces.

VOGUE   AUGUST 2001

VOGUE   SEPTEMBER 2001

VOGUE   MARCH 2000

armchair. There's nothing wrong with veneered wood furniture, but check the quality; some cheap veneers are very fragile. If possible, choose solid wood for a table that will see lots of use. Opt for real metal instead of a metal-effect finish, which may chip.

The key to choosing successful living-room essentials is versatility. Any of the major building blocks will involve a substantial outlay, even a budget couch. So you need to assume that when, in five years' time, the living-room walls are repainted another color, the furniture will still be going strong, though small details may need tweaking. It's therefore important to pick designs that can reflect fresh looks. Pick sofas with pretty legs and an elegant silhouette, giving you the option of choosing upholstery or slipcovers. Simple, inexpensive composite-board or wood pieces can be repainted in different colors. And think of smaller items—console tables or a side chair—as the equivalents of those skirts and slacks that mix and match with the key suit jacket. If they are attractive in their own right, they can also be moved around the house for visual variety.

In terms of design, there are certain failsafe styles for the living room. For upholstery, many classics are still the best. You can't go far wrong with a wing chair, a small Victorian armchair, a squared-off Knole couch, or a Howard-style sofa, all of which not only boast a great outline, but also look good with both antiques and contemporary pieces. For a more modern look, the boxy sofa, cube armchair, or L-shaped modular sofa are all set to stay for the foreseeable future. Ignore clumsy or overly fussy designs with puffy pillows. When choosing tables or cabinets, stick to simple styling in quality materials, remembering that a mix of curvy and rectangular shapes won't tie a room down to any particular style or decade. And don't get hung up on classics at the expense of indulging your personal style. Let that shine through in one or two unusual pieces.

Once the essential furniture choices are made, it is crucial to realize them in as neutral a palette as possible. Choose upholstery in cool tones, from white to deep graphite, and furniture in wood, metal, or rattan. Then apply this palette to smaller items, from ceramic lamp bases to stone platters, glass vases, and oak photo frames. Cover windows with white roll-up or Roman shades, or wooden or metal Venetian blinds, keeping your options open for luxurious curtain treatments later. If there are wooden floorboards, consider sisal, jute, or neutral-colored wool rugs. There are two

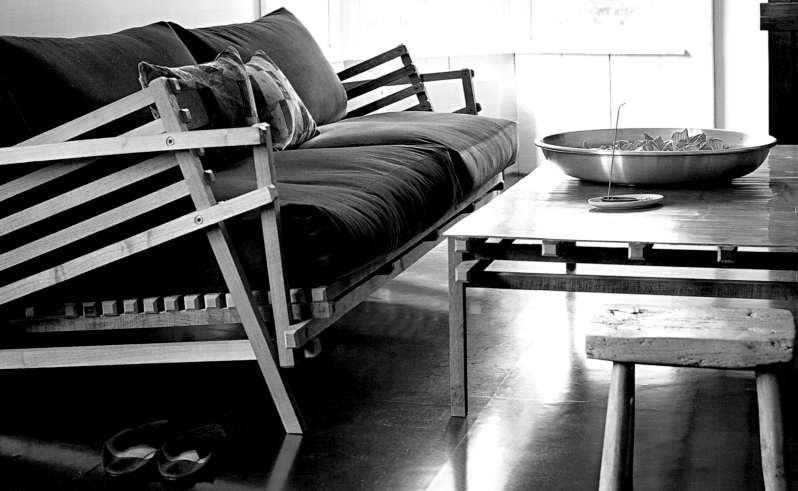

This page and opposite In most living rooms, it is invariably the sofa that becomes the natural point of focus, not only because it is the most heavily used piece, but because it takes up the most space. So it's crucial to be happy with the style you have—if necessary buying afresh—because it will set the entire decorative tone of a room. Think carefully about upholstery. If your other furniture tends toward hard finishes, you can get away with upholstering your major piece in a distinctive color *(see opposite page)*. If there are a number of other soft-textured items, from rugs to other upholstered pieces, stick to white or neutral fabrics *(this page)*, to allow plenty of scope for changing accessories.

If the room is very pared down, whatever you add in terms of ornaments will attract more, not less, attention, so choose wisely.

reasons for creating a neutral skeleton. Quite apart from the fact that it provides a perfect backdrop for bright and more luxurious accessories, it actively detracts from an obvious trend or date of furniture. A wing chair in dark paisley is "period," whereas the same chair upholstered in white cotton is simply a pretty shape that blends with other styles.

At this point, bring color and pattern into play. In the same way that we all have bold or pastel-colored basic clothes among our whites and neutrals (where's the fun otherwise?), apply the same principle to the living room. Plan to have some key pieces in color, too. Whether that's a single large piece, like an armchair upholstered in tangerine denim, or several smaller items, such as shell-pink occasional tables, the point to remember

is that the colors should be easy and inexpensive to change. So look out for sale-bargain fabrics or furniture that can be repainted. If a patterned or colored piece is to last, make sure you love it in its own right as opposed to tying it into a complete coordinated scheme. One armchair upholstered in green chintz will look good with a white couch, or—five years on—with a gray one; it is only when the chintz has been matched to other elements such as chairs and curtains that problems arise.

When dressing up the living room at the basics stage, allow for as many inexpensive accessories as possible. With a selection of glass, metal, and ceramic vases, you can create myriad looks, from using them as vases to arranging a still life. The same principle goes for plain photo frames, platters, and candlesticks. If the room is very pared down, whatever you add in terms of ornaments will attract more, not less, attention, so choose wisely. Scale accessories up, make them quirky, so there is a definite focus of attention.

This page and opposite **By definition, living-room basics are simple shapes in neutral tones. Having amassed the essential items, those with a naturally pared-down style will want to stop right there, steering clear of anything so flamboyant as a velvet cushion. That's fine. But it's nice to know that if funds are limited, you have the flexibility to upgrade the quality of your pieces slowly, without wavering from your chosen style. All the pieces in this room are top quality, a mix of twentieth-century classics, linen chair covers, and hand-thrown ceramics. If you can't afford these luxuries, start with a copycat look from the chain stores and gradually work up to them.**

living room
real list

Sofa and/or armchairs; upholstered *(neutral cotton, denim, linen hopsack)*

Side chair *(wood, metal, plastic)*

Coffee and/or side tables *(wood, metal, painted board)*

Book shelf or unit *(painted board, wood, metal)*

Mirror *(wood, metal, or molded plaster)*

Rug *(neutral wool or natural fibers)*

Reading/task lights *(ceramic or metallic bases; card, paper, or metal shades)*

Paintings and artworks *(painted canvases, watercolors, photographs)*

Vases, platters, bowls *(glass, ceramic, stone, wood)*

Pillows, throws *(colored or neutral cotton, linen)*

Wastebasket, storage baskets *(metal, rattan, wood)*

Candlesticks and holders *(glass, galvanized metal, ceramic)*

Left and below left **At first** glance, this is a glamorous, even fashionable, living room. Yet look closer at its components, and the simple, adaptable building blocks are clear: the neutral, contemporary couch, plainly styled coffee table, and wooden slatted blinds. Swap the silk curtains, embroidered antique pillows, and serious art for plain white cotton drapes, linen pillow covers, and a simple wood-framed mirror; and the room would still look good. The trick is that the luxurious accessories that stamp the decorative tone are easily added to or taken away from the basics. Get into the habit of analyzing well-composed rooms in interiors magazines or while staying in hotel rooms, to see how the layers from basics to luxuries are built up.

living room luxuries

It's up to you whether the luxuries you add to the living room are visual or practical, or a mix of both; but before you decide, think about how you use the room. If yours is a family home, are the children/pets allowed into the living room and if so, how much time do you want to devote to keeping it pristine? Do you entertain frequently? Is it a priority to provide lots of extra seating? Or to put together a perfect room full of exquisite pieces to impress visitors?

In practical terms, you might first concentrate on moving beyond those initial building blocks—sofa, tables, and so on—by gradually acquiring furniture that's not strictly necessary, yet adds comfort and visual zest. This might include a pretty desk, a retro drinks cabinet or a sleek purpose-built cabinet to hide the stereo and video and give the room more polish. A pair of side or carver chairs is a useful extra, since they provide additional seating for guests, as well as cutting a sharper and more decorative silhouette than an upholstered couch ever can. Provided your basic furniture "wardrobe" is in place, these are pieces of furniture you can add, year after year, so the room evolves gradually. It's for this reason, at the outset, that it's worth knowing what available spare floor space the room has. Shopping for these pieces then becomes a fun, ad hoc process, adding an extra frisson to browsing antique or secondhand stores.

Left Whatever your luxuries, give
thought to showing them off to
their best advantage. This living
room has a multi-level hanging
system, so the art displayed can be
changed around easily; Victorian
picture rails are an alternative. If
you want to draw deliberate
attention to a special work of art or
piece of furniture, experiment by
trying out different positions in the
room to find the optimum location.
Choose a focal point, as well as a
spot where both natural and
artificial light highlight the piece,
but make sure its quality is also up
to such close scrutiny.

Above Keep up a constant search
for pleasing exotic, ethnic, or
antique decorative objects.

Now is also the time to consider where and how you might add to the basics. You should be able to use every inch of the living room to its best advantage, not just the area where the couch and TV are situated. This might mean adding an extra armchair and floor lamp to create a reading area, or having enough occasional tables so the occupant of every chair has room to place drinks and books. In addition to the essential reading lamp, think about adding more mood and task lighting, such as picture lights or wall sconces with decorative shades. If you like lounging on the floor, consider floor cushions, cubes, or a leather beanbag.

This is also a good time to expand your style options and be a touch more radical. If you have stuck to simple classics initially, branch out into more exotic choices. Boxy, simple side tables could

This page and opposite **In composing a room with a look of understated luxury, rather than flamboyance, it is often the details that take simple, pared-down styling to more glamorous heights. In this drawing room, extras such as the rug's contrasting border, throw with narrow leather trim, and gilded decorative bowls give a polished finish to the neutral basics of contemporary sofa and plain side tables. If a room seems in danger of having too many similar shapes—cubes and straight lines, say—the more fluid curves of a retro or antique piece of furniture can add just the right amount of contrast.**

This page If your priority is to splash out on contemporary designer furniture to make a decorative statement, choose a smaller piece such as a side chair rather than a big item like a sofa. This way, in years to come you can update the living room with a different chair—perhaps retro instead of modern—and the statement piece can create new looks elsewhere in the house. This couch is a perfect example of the "colored neutrals"—sludgy off-blues, greens, or lilacs—that cross the border between neutral and pastel colors, and also endure well for major living-room purchases.

Opposite page, left Decorating in stages: heavy linen curtains, a sparkling chandelier, and antique side table have been added slowly to this room's original purchases of sofa and Roman shades.

Opposite page, right With basic white-linen-covered chairs and couch already in place, this room awaits the addition of understated luxuries such as white linen drapes and selected decorative antiques.

be supplemented with a lacquered Chinese trunk; a pair of neutrally upholstered armchairs by a gilded Louis XV side chair covered in eau de nil silk. Enjoy searching out special pieces and expanding your style horizons, even if you don't plan to buy yet. If you normally shop in antique stores, visit some contemporary furniture showrooms; if pared-down style is second nature to you, consider boudoir-chic accessories. However confident you are of your particular look, it's good for everyone to explore new avenues occasionally.

If you are happy with your existing choice of furniture, you may simply want to upgrade certain pieces. When considering sofa fabrics, consider practicality first. Pale colors look fabulous but mark easily. Luxurious upholstery options that also wear well include wool mixes, linen, or chenille. For chairs, silk, satin, or suede make good options. Covering pillows or a small chair in a fabric you adore will look almost as good as an entire couch in the fabric, but is much less expensive. Lamp bases are easy to upgrade. A plain glass or metal base can look ultra-simple with a drum shade, or more elaborate with a pleated silk or molded paper shade.

It's also possible to give a new twist to an existing arrangement of furniture simply by adding one or two quality items. The addition of a leather-upholstered desk or an imposing modern oil on canvas can instantly impart a more sophisticated timbre to neutral cotton upholstery and simple wood furniture. Many contemporary furniture designers have reworked classic designs in unusual fabrics, from a console table in faux snakeskin to a butler's-tray-style occasional table with chrome legs, so examine these options, too.

This page and opposite **If you are drawn to more obviously flamboyant detailing, there's an art to combining it successfully. Any one of the glamorous pieces shown here, used individually, would transform a classic, neutral living room into a luxurious retreat. Yet it's possible to use several exotic items together without tiring too soon of a truly opulent look. The key is to dress up each separately, rather than create a matching set. In years to come, a white leather-upholstered chair would look as good with this purple velvet sofa as the gray and gilded wrought-iron chair, or the polished-steel coffee table could be replaced with a limestone-and-steel style. To get maximum mileage from investment luxury buys, choose pieces that can mix and match as well as your neutral basics do.**

It's also comforting to remember that if funds are limited, it's always possible to add the odd luxurious extra to a living room without spending a fortune. There is a plethora of exquisite accessories to consider, from velvet or sequined scatter cushions to suede seating cubes, animal-skin rugs, hand-blown glass lamp bases, and satin throws. You can tailor what you buy to your budget: versions of varying quality, but equally good looks, are available both in chain stores and in designer shops.

Once the furniture and smaller accessories are assured, remember that all the best living rooms have a "wow" factor that draws everyone's attention. Plan for this, but

It's also possible to give a new twist to an existing arrangement of furniture simply by adding one or two quality items.

choose an accessory, rather than a piece of furniture, to do the job. It can help to leave investing in this piece until the room is almost completed. The item may be something on a large scale—a floor-to-ceiling gilded mirror or a crystal chandelier—or a custommade rug woven to your own design. Alternatively, you may find that having rearranged your living room into a neutral, more accommodating backdrop, there is now space for something that didn't quite fit before. Be that a rosewood piano, or a portrait of your great-grandfather, you—and everyone else—can enjoy it again now.

living room
wish list

Armchair, stool, daybed; upholstered *(velvet, silk, linen, leather, moleskin)*

Rugs, limited edition or custommade *(faux fur, needlepoint, antique)*

Sideboard, console, desk; designer or retro *(leather, mirrored, veneered, lacquered)*

Chandelier

Contemporary designer floor lamp *(porcelain or silk shades; metal base)*

Mood lighting *(antique or custommade bases; silk, paper, or beaded shades)*

Pillow covers *(satin, linen, embroidered, beaded)*

Throws *(velvet, mohair, cashmere, satin)*

Platters, bowls, vases *(gilded, porcelain, blown glass, hand-painted)*

Scented candles and incense holders *(soapstone, granite, hand-blown glass)*

Dress curtains *(silk, satin, linen, silk chiffon)*

eating rooms

Give due attention to everyday eating essentials—and the tables and chairs that you sit on—and you'll be guaranteed a hard-wearing, versatile dining kit to last for years. Then concentrate on assembling a wardrobe of exotic or sophisticated dining accessories to turn entertaining and parties into creative events.

This page **If your taste naturally inclines toward rustic or ethnic looks, make a stylistic virtue out of choosing a very simple table and set of chairs made from textured wood planks or rough woven rattan. However raw the component materials, try to select a style that possesses an element of sophistication—here, it is the elegantly crisscrossed table legs— so there is the option to dress it up with beaten metals, exotic flowers, or unusual glassware.**

Left, right, and below **One of the most enduring style formulas is to combine a traditional wooden table with contemporary plastic or metal chairs. Depending on your budget, the possibilities range from a country pine table to a simple yet sophisticated walnut or cherrywood example; and from budget stacking chairs to modern designer classics. The confident mix of two different styles sets the tone, allowing you to experiment with contrasting plain and funky tableware, as well as keeping options open to add contemporary artwork—or perhaps an antique side table—later on.**

eating room basics

In today's frenetic world, we should all regularly take time to sit down and eat with family or friends. A well-proportioned table and comfortable chairs are necessities, not luxuries, and should go right to the top of your real list. Everything in a dining room must be hard-working, because this is a high-activity area. Yet the decorative choices you make are crucial, too. When not in use, a dining table and chairs take up plenty of room and need to please the eye; when they are set for meals, they are the center of attention.

Ideally, you should make an early investment in a beautiful, quality table that will last you a lifetime. If there are no funds for that now, at least make sure your table is the right size and height (the correct table height is 28–30 inches). Choose one that sits six to eight people and plan for extra guests or an expanding family by selecting a style with hinged ends or extending central sections.

When choosing a style, go for one that offers maximum potential for dressing the table up or down. You won't lose if you pick a design with pared-down styling in a medium-toned solid wood, which will

If you can't change your chairs, have a unifying set of slipcovers made from inexpensive muslin to last until you can upgrade.

go with everything. If the table is in the kitchen, you can choose a more rustic or utilitarian style, but make sure it has pretty legs, so that with a white tablecloth and more formal tableware it can take on a more sophisticated look. Always look at a table with a cloth on it before you buy; some leg designs look odd poking out at the bottom.

Chairs are a classic investment buy, too, because you need them in bulk. You have several choices. If your table is a good design, it's easier to pair it with trendy, inexpensive polypropylene, lacquered steel, or rattan chairs than it is to mix good chairs with an unimpressive table. If you can't change your chairs, have a unifying set of slipcovers made from inexpensive muslin to last until you can upgrade. For a traditional look, a mix-and-match set of secondhand chairs, from classic ladderbacks to schoolroom styles, are practical and visually adaptable. When buying new chairs, figure out the maximum number you need. If space is tight, consider stacking or folding styles, or choose a very neutral wood or rattan design so spare chairs will blend easily into another room.

If your eating area is in a separate dining room, it's essential to have storage for tableware, glasses, and linens. Decades ago, the formal or decorative sideboard or hutch was an expected

Left Ignore good overhead lighting at your peril; it is an essential component even in the most elementary of dining rooms. Try to install a dimmer switch, so you can control the mood in the room, from bright at breakfast time to seductive during parties. Try to choose a light that will contrast nicely with the chairs and tables you already have. For example, this oversized industrial design is a wonderful foil for the extreme simplicity of the chairs and table shown here. What you spend on the light fixture is immaterial (inexpensive giant paper globe shades still look as good today as they did in the Seventies). Instead of thinking of cost, concentrate on a quirky, eye-catching, oversized style that makes a statement.
Opposite page, left and far left Restaurant classics, such as plain wine glasses, bistro flatware, and plain white plates, are perfect dining staples that can be mixed with decorative or plain pieces.

Opposite page If you are investing in a good, long-lasting dining table, particularly one that will be situated in a kitchen/dining room, make sure it will fulfill a number of different functions. The clever stools around this table mean it's ideal for family meals on the run as well as acting as a kitchen preparation table and a generous work surface that doubles as a desk. The harder-working the table will have to be, the more important it is to pick one made from robust materials—ideal choices are polished, lacquered, or scrubbed wood surfaces. The best examples of reproduction antique country wood tables are already nicely distressed, so a few more scratches won't matter.

Right Chairs aren't the only seating option. Consider benches, stools, or old church pews. Stools are a good choice if you want to the eye to be drawn to the table silhouette, since they sit so discreetly below the tabletop.

investment. These days, you can treat this form of storage as a way of adding informality or modernity to a dining room. The options include a low, lean composite-board sideboard with sliding doors, a secondhand armoire with shelves, or an industrial-style metal open shelf unit. If you progress to a more "grown-up" dining-room look in later years, this storage can be reused elsewhere.

Tableware can involve as much or as little investment as you choose; what matters is that everything you choose is neutral, and that the quantities are correct. In buying a new set of tableware, whether glasses or plates, be generous with your quantities. Using the same principle as you might for clothes, aim for some in the cupboard, some on the table, and some in the dishwasher. Is there enough for entertaining up to your maximum preferred numbers, too? Add to those initial principles of neutral colors and simple, classic styling the need for dual-purpose tableware. Bowls should hold cereal, dessert, salad, or soup, while glasses should be versatile enough to hold wine, water, or simple flowers, and serving plates deep enough for salads, fruit, or pasta. Choosing one color—white or cream—means it's easier to amass tableware from different sources that will still combine together well.

Spare a thought for practicality. Follow the basic rules when shopping for new tableware. Read the labels and buy nothing for everyday that isn't microwave- and dishwasher-safe and (in the case of table linen or mats) machine-washable. If an item needs to function efficiently (pitchers and teapots, for example), ask to try it out with water in the store. A good-looking style, unfortunately, doesn't always guarantee great performance. Widen your net beyond the mall for tableware suppliers (there are useful suggestions in Suppliers, see pages 138–139). For everyday tableware, try catering suppliers and mail order; for robust, if un-matching, silver flatware or napkin rings, explore thrift stores; for everyday linen tablecloths, source antique textile specialists.

Even at the building-block stage, it's important to amass some colorful basics and more exotic accessories. Put together a wardrobe of inexpensive candle holders, glass or ceramic vases, funky tablemats, and serving dishes or pitchers. Keep an eye out for sale bargains such as sets of colorful plates or napkins, and look beyond conventional homeware stores. Ethnic shops (woven bowls and mats), garden supply stores (galvanized containers), and fabric stores (linen and dishtowel fabrics) are all good hunting grounds.

eating room
real list

Table, preferably extendable *(painted board, wood, laminate)*

Dining chairs *(wood, metal, plastic, rattan)*

Hutch/sideboard *(wood and glass, painted board, metal)*

Light fixture, modern or industrial style *(paper, metal, glass)*

Tablecloths, napkins *(white, colored, checked, or striped cotton)*

Table mats *(raffia, rubber, cork, plastic, cotton, slate)*

Glasses; tumblers and wine
(clear, bubbled, ribbed)

Pitchers and serving platters, assorted sizes *(glass, earthenware, wood, metal)*

Flatware, serving spoons *(stainless steel, antique silver-plate)*

Tableware; large and side plates, bowls *(white/neutral earthenware or glass)*

Coffee cups *(white or neutral china)*

Vases, candle holders *(galvanized metal, glass, ceramic)*

Opposite page **Upholstered dining chairs are always a luxury: not only are they more comfortable, but the fabric covering adds an instant air of polish to a simple, pared-down table. These days, there's a huge variety of styles to choose, from the squared-off contemporary shape of models such as these, to reproductions of classic silhouettes such as Georgian, Gothic, and Chippendale chairs. If you are struggling with a set of the latter, and they don't seem to fit with a contemporary table, consider how very different they would look reupholstered in a sleek modern fabric such as plain suede, linen, or moleskin, rather than traditional brocade or silk stripe.**

Right and below right **The ultimate luxury is a custommade or designer dining table that makes a real design statement. If you're getting something made to order, and you entertain a lot, expand the dimensions so it can accommodate twelve people.**

eating room luxuries

Traditionally there has always been a distinction in the dining room between "best" and "everyday" china and silverware, often resulting in overly formal dinner parties. Thankfully, this is now outmoded, and these days it's more important to choose luxurious extras that add sparkle or make a design statement. Tailor the luxuries you choose to your lifestyle. If you have lots of parties, the emphasis should be on creating choice for varying looks; if personal comfort matters, invest in upholstered chairs and well-balanced flatware that is pleasurable to hold. Think about maintenance, but don't discount special items such as crystal wine glasses or bone-handled flatware just because they need to be hand-washed. There's a certain delicious pleasure in caring for precious objects.

If you can afford your dream dining table now, think carefully about materials and design. Are you a tablecloth person? If not, the style of the table matters much more: the silhouette, materials, and practicality of the tabletop, in particular. If you want a modern design, find a designer you like and invest in what should, in time, become a designer classic. A less radical choice is to choose a mix of contemporary and traditional materials: a glass top with wooden legs, for example. Pick designs in neutral shades such as white rather than acid-colored laminates. Classic antique choices that always look

good include French fruitwood country tables, a long oak table, or iron legs with a marble top. Steer clear of highly polished, very ornate mahogany designs, which don't mix well with contemporary tableware or chairs.

To give yourself maximum decorative flexibility, don't buy a set of dining chairs that obviously matches your table. You will saddle yourself with such a specific look that it will be expensive to change if your tastes alter. Think of chairs as decorative "dressing-up" accessories for the table. If funds allow, you can't go wrong buying real or reproduction design-classic chairs, from Arne Jacobsen's 3107 chair to Philippe Starck's Lord Yo armchair. Check whether a design is ongoing for a few years; this way, you can buy two chairs per year or swoop on sale bargains.

For others, a set of pretty antique chairs is the ultimate luxury, though it's rare (and expensive) to find a matching set of eight or more. Alternatively, opt for collecting slight variations on a period chair type or get copies made to match the antique chairs you already possess. Upholstered dining chairs can be the ultimate in comfort and sophisticated good looks. If you can afford them now, but only in budget brushed cotton, there's time to save for more luxurious suede, linen, or cashmere upholstery at a later date. A set of slipcovers, in a dramatic pattern, also brings a decorative twist to a pared-down dining room and gives maximum mileage to the upholstery option.

When choosing special tableware, consider the choices. Those who love subtle luxury but simple styles may want merely to upgrade their neutral basics, swapping chunky white earthenware plates for fine porcelain or machine-made wine

Left and above Although modern chairs can look great with an antique table, the opposite rarely works. If you own or have chosen a set of antique chairs, it's best to team them with an antique table in a similar wood. Concentrate on finding antique-chair styles that are really pretty, featuring curved or caned backs, painted detail, or an unusual inlay. This not only means that spare chairs can look very decorative when situated elsewhere, perhaps in a hall or a living room, but that they are adaptable to a variety of looks. The perfect antique chair should look as at home at a kitchen table for an easy lunchtime table setting as they do at a more formal gathering, with damask tablecloth and antique glass and silverware. Pick a neat, high-backed design, with attractively shaped legs, and you also have the opportunity to give the chairs new looks with a slipcover, too.

Once you are assured of the basic and special things for your table, look out for exotic accessories and "props" with which to dress the table.

glasses for hand-blown crystal. There's also the kind of "best" tableware our grandparents had in their cabinets. Anyone who has compiled a wedding list will know that the market is flooded with traditional bone-china dinner sets, cut-glass fruit bowls, and damask tablecloths. It's nice to amass a few of these things for the odd occasion when formality is called for; equally, because many are beautifully crafted, they are heirlooms you can pass on. Not everyone likes traditional styling. If this is the case, investigate established companies who have employed young designers to create trendy updates of tableware that is still made by traditional methods.

Once you are assured of the basic and special things for your table, look out for exotic accessories with which to dress the table. Some will be expensive, such as gilded water glasses or silk table runners; others will be fashion items such as sequined napkin rings or stainless-steel espresso cups and saucers. Depending on the occasion, you can have a casual dinner-party setting with white plates and scarlet wine glasses, or layer different textures and finishes for a flamboyant effect. Search out unusual extras, such as silver-plated chopsticks, funky cocktail glasses, an antique punch bowl, and so on. The only limit, ultimately, is your storage space.

Opposite page This dining room perfectly demonstrates the way in which classics, basics, and luxuries work so well together. The simple dining table is a classic that will last for years, while the luxurious designer chairs add comfort and a fashionable twist. Combined with the basic white paper lampshade, catering glassware and white china, the room looks fresh and simple. But it's the exotic vase with unusual pods and the distressed secondhand cabinet that introduce the all-important eccentric element.

This page It's a high-maintenance look, but white slipcovered chairs and a blond wood table are the ultimate blank canvas if you want to dress up the table with vivid colors and bold, oversized pieces.

eating room
wish list

Table, antique or designer *(solid wood; metal and glass)*

Dining chairs; retro, antique, contemporary *(antique wood or upholstered)*

Sideboard or serving table *(lacquer, wood, wood veneer)*

Hanging light fixture *(crystal chandelier, ultra-modern fixture)*

Tablecloths, napkins *(white linen or damask, bright silk table runners)*

Placemats *(linen, lacquer, beaded)*

Glasses; wine, champagne, water *(hand-blown crystal, colored glass, antique)*

Pitchers, candlesticks, platters *(crystal, colored glass, porcelain, silver-plated, metal)*

Flatware, serving spoons *(silver-plated, mother of pearl, bone-handled)*

Unusual sets of dessert bowls or coffee cups *(crackleglaze, metallic, hand-painted, antique)*

Napkin rings, place-card holders *(silver, enameled, pewter, bejeweled)*

% LINEN
E WASH 60°C / 140°F
ARK COLOURS SEPARATELY
L AFFECT SHADE

kitchens

The kitchen is more than a workroom. Nowadays, it has to be a design statement, entertaining space, and action zone all rolled into one. So the successful kitchen must combine simple good looks with supreme functionality. Get the equipment right now, and it won't date, let you down, or wear out for years.

kitchen basics

In recent decades, the kitchen has become both a fashion statement and a status symbol. Yet so much attention is focused on the design of the cabinets, the finish of the countertop, and the glossy built-in appliances, that little thought goes to the bits and pieces you place within. These are the items that matter most, from a comfortable kitchen stool to good mixing bowls and a china coffeepot that pours well. A great-looking kitchen is so easily ruined by inappropriate choices. And it's vital that the cooking utensils and equipment perform well, however infrequently you cook. So

be ruthless with your lists. Think both about the things that will be out on show, and the real basics that hide in the cabinets.

Humble though it seems, it makes perfect sense to start your lists with daily cooking equipment. Use the real lists as a prompt, and look at cookbooks to see what equipment serious cooks consider essential. Always buy the best you can afford, because it won't date and is designed for constant use. It's better to have an enduring capsule collection of great kit that you add to than quantities of useless gadgets. The kitchen is one

Above, left and right **In a kitchen that features open-plan storage, the equipment needs to possess decorative appeal as well as functionality. Here the concept of plain basics, from enamel pitchers to white plates, is interpreted with a deliberately rustic bias. The rough-and-ready nature of the accessories, in turn, means that a diverse mix of freestanding pieces, from a retro fridge to a workman's stool, look surprisingly good together.**

This page It's perfectly possible
to plan a basic yet good-looking
kitchen on a modest budget. When
choosing seating, it's sensible to
start off with something as simple
as folding garden chairs. They cost
little, won't date, provide versatile
seating, and can eventually be put
out to pasture in the backyard
when you upgrade. Multifunctional
furniture is also excellent. These
seating blocks can be reused as
coffee tables in a living room, and
the slate-topped dining table
doubles as an additional food
preparation surface.

Look at serious cookbooks to see what equipment professional cooks consider essential. Buy the best you can afford because it won't date.

room where it pays to visit specialized kitchen outlets or a good department store, rather than buy chain-store basics that have good looks but may be lacking in practicality.

Tailor the lists to your individual requirements. If you know you're an undisciplined cook, allow for lots of wooden spoons and several colanders; wash-as-they-go individuals can cope with one of everything. Don't try to match everything to your current kitchen. If you're buying a mix of traditional basics (such as a ceramic mixing bowl) with catering-quality saucepans, you're on the right track. Cooking utensils do not need to be trendy.

Most kitchens these days incorporate built-in appliances, but if you are moving house or planning a new design, consider freestanding styles. There is an increasing choice of characterful, retro-inspired fridges and stainless-steel catering-style ovens, which act as a fashion element in an otherwise sterile row of cabinets. In terms of the investment value, it's comforting to know that you can move and take a favorite appliance with you.

Small electrical appliances must work well and look good too. Opinions will vary as to the basics. To the ubiquitous coffeemaker and toaster, a foodie might add a juicer, mixer, and blender as essentials. Do you want a specific appliance for each task, or is one all-singing, all-dancing food processor more your style? Whatever you choose should be easy to use and to clean. It should also be accessible, kept close to hand on the counter. Therefore style matters. Pick a classic design in stainless steel or white.

Spare a thought for the Cinderellas of the kitchen: the dishwashing bowl, the trash can. We have to have them, so choose an appealing design. In making a stylistic statement in a truly basic kitchen, go for

Opposite page **In a serious cook's kitchen, investment in classic gadgets such as a quality mixer and blender is completely justified. Their shiny good looks are the only decoration an essentially functional workspace needs.**

Left and above **In kitchens where the units are sleek and pared down, the furniture must perform the "dressing-up" role. Instead of matching a kitchen table and chairs to the cabinets (making it difficult when you move on or change kitchens), take a cue from the predominant material in the room. Here, smooth wood on the cabinets is complemented by a contrasting rough floorboard tabletop and retro-style wooden chairs.**

classic designs such as a galvanized-metal trash can and traditional enamel bread box. In a minimalist kitchen where there a few things on show, take the time to find funky examples.

Choose kitchen furniture with care, since it needs wipe-down surfaces and a certain flexibility, particularly if the kitchen doubles as a dining or family room. Good options include tables on wheels, folding chairs, and storage trolleys. Look for simplicity of style so an individual piece can be reused even if you change your kitchen. There are choices here. You might obviate the need to choose a classic piece by buying cheap, colored plastic or galvanized-metal chairs, accepting that you may replace them in five years' time. Do invest in a decent food-preparation trolley or kitchen table, however. A sturdy zinc-topped table or a solid wood butcher's block on wheels will last you through several kitchen incarnations.

Few of us hang pictures in our kitchens, preferring a pinboard or—at most—a no-nonsense clock. Yet think carefully about "dressing up" the kitchen. An old clock or battered laboratory stool mixed with modern cupboards, or a distressed pine hutch teamed with limestone countertops, can pave the way for a mix-and-match collection of equipment and make a kitchen seem more lived-in. Think, too, about how smaller items, such as storage jars, will look with the rest of the room. Don't have too many little things lined up against a splashback. Scaling things up creates more impact: a big bread box, large tea and coffee canisters, and an oversized wicker basket for vegetables will hit the right note.

This page and opposite **This room is proof that a true working kitchen, well equipped with basics, can still have a strong, decorative appeal and be the sum of its parts, not its cabinet doors. Although the kitchen appears disarmingly casual at first glance, the essentials are neatly categorized and arranged so everything is easily at hand. However utilitarian a kitchen is, there is always room for a little dressing up. The glittering inset tiles provide a quirky touch.**

kitchen *real list*

Kitchen table or work-station *(wood, stainless-steel, or zinc-topped)*

Kitchen chairs, stools, or benches *(galvanized metal, powder-coated steel, wood, vinyl-covered)*

Toaster; coffeemaker

Trash can *(galvanized metal, plastic, stainless steel)*

Saucepans, skillet, wok, colander

Spoons, spatulas; whisks, tongs, and ladle *(wood; stainless steel)*

Knives and scissors *(stainless steel)*

Roasting pans and cookie sheets

Casserole/ovenproof gratin dishes

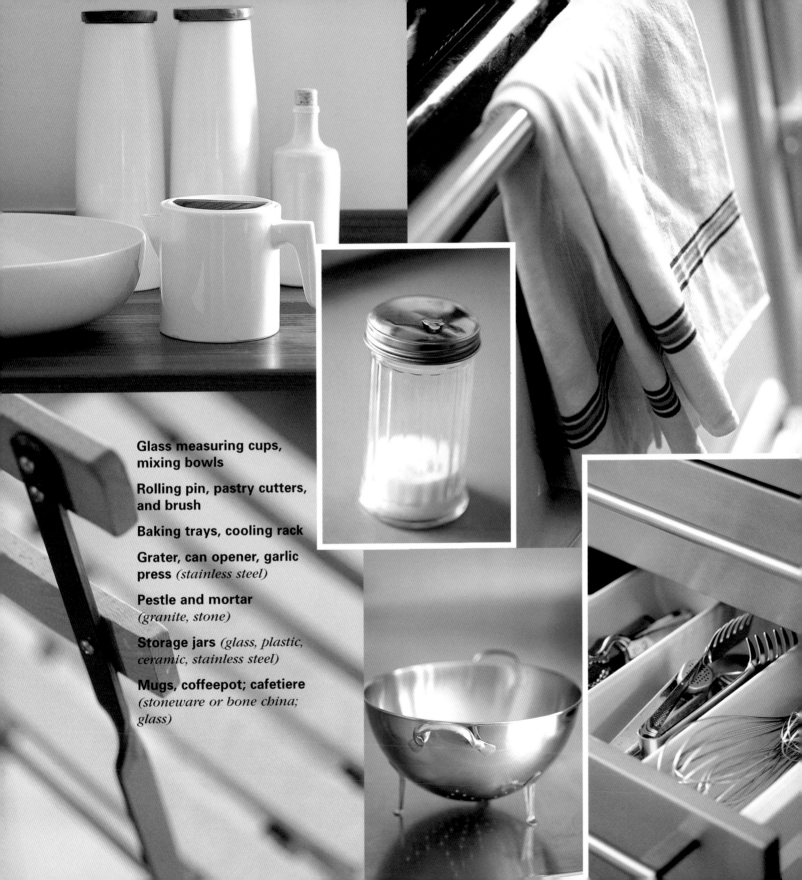

Glass measuring cups, mixing bowls

Rolling pin, pastry cutters, and brush

Baking trays, cooling rack

Grater, can opener, garlic press *(stainless steel)*

Pestle and mortar *(granite, stone)*

Storage jars *(glass, plastic, ceramic, stainless steel)*

Mugs, coffeepot; cafetiere *(stoneware or bone china; glass)*

kitchen luxuries

In an ideal world, our kitchens should be a direct reflection of our lifestyles. A busy person should invest in an efficient microwave and a huge freezer for lots of quick meals, while a domestic goddess will want plenty of decent pots and pans. But that's not always the case. Too many of us view the kitchen as a design statement and end up with a room and equipment that looks great but doesn't cater to our individual needs. When adding to the basics, the fundamental questions to ask are how important cooking is, will you be entertaining in the room, and is the mood to be cozy or trendy?

If cooking is the primary activity, then there's a raft of extra equipment beyond the basics that makes life easier. There's a difference between unnecessary gadgets and useful specifics that suit your culinary preferences, such as an asparagus boiler, fish steamer or blowtorch. Alternatively, you might want a more varied choice of basic items: cake pans in numerous shapes, for example, or twice the number of casserole dishes.

If your luxury is upgrading from basic equipment, seek out top-quality materials. The best pans are copper, heavy-gauge aluminum, or stainless steel. Casserole dishes should be cast enamel and chopping boards hardwood, while kitchen tools—from ladles to a garlic press—are best in stainless steel. Roasting pans should be stainless steel or enamel, measuring cups made from glass, and the pestle and mortar from granite

Opposite page **With its instantly cozy appeal and curved lines, the range is still considered by many to be the ultimate luxury in the kitchen, even when it's used in conjunction with a modern built-in stove. Like all good classic pieces of furniture, it somehow fits in both a country-style kitchen or with a streamlined modern look. There's a certain playful luxury in choosing**
an unexpected fashionable color, or you can play safe with a neutral such as cream or black.
Above **In a kitchen/dining room, there is as much fun to be had choosing one-off, retro, or ethnic tableware to go with basics, as in an eating room. Patterns, from Sixties prints to contemporary abstracts, are an ideal way to dress up an otherwise pared-down kitchen.**

or stone. Only once you are assured of quality materials should you look at the style. Classic shapes are always winners, with the exception, perhaps, of saucepans: in a minimal kitchen, pick ones with tapered handles and sleek lines.

No one can deny the pleasure of visiting someone and being served fresh espresso from a steaming machine. Such gadgets may be expensive, but they are efficient and perform a decorative function, too. Increasingly, design classics, from toasters to juice squeezers, come not just in chrome or stainless-steel finishes, but in a choice of pastel or bright colors. Pick the finish that most pleases you, not the one that matches your current kitchen. Stainless steel will eventually go out of fashion, whereas bold red or bright yellow will always look stylish. Apart from the classics, consider other gadgets that might appeal. An ice-cream or bread maker may be the serious cook's idea of heaven.

If the kitchen doubles as an entertaining space, with a dining table and chairs, the furniture also needs to fuse style and practicality. You can't afford to indulge in upholstery, particularly if there are kids around—the likelihood of smears and smudges is too high. The first decision will be whether or not to match the furniture to the cabinets. Try not to, particularly if you are planning

Opposite page and left **Whether the cabinets are from the mall or designer creations, in a simple kitchen there is much decorative mileage to be had from the addition of just a few sleek, shiny, stainless-steel gadgets and appliances. They needn't all be electrical. Other choices might include Philippe Starck's "Juicy Salif" lemon squeezer on legs or assorted Alessi design classics. But before you buy, do be sure that these pieces are truly user-friendly as well as looking good.**

The first decision will be whether or not to match the furniture to the cabinets. Try not to, particularly if you are planning to move or upgrade the kitchen at a later date.

Left **Just because it's a hard-working room doesn't mean that you can't put great art or classic furniture into a kitchen. A few carefully chosen items will lift the functionality and facelessness of items such as a giant stainless-steel fridge, and can always be used elsewhere in the house if you tire of them in the kitchen.**
Below left **Decorative touches do make a difference. Look for unusual containers that dress up everyday substances, from dried herbs and spices to salad-dressing containers.**
Opposite page **The more open-plan the kitchen and the storage, the more editing must take place. In addition to providing the perfect equipment for setting the table, the pure white plates, glassware, and stainless-steel pots and pans also create the perfect—and only—decoration in this kitchen.**

to move or upgrade the kitchen at a later date. For tables, choose hard-working yet sophisticated surfaces that work well in most kitchens, such as marble, granite, solid wood, or stainless steel; look for designer chairs or stools with chrome detailing or in neutral laminates and high-spec plastics. Sophisticated versions of utility furniture are good choices in a kitchen/dining room—go for minimalist wooden benches, designer galvanized-metal chairs, or a stainless-steel-topped table.

For the tableware, the same rules apply as for eating rooms: keep to a neutral skeleton with white, gray, and stone tones and lots of glass. It's particularly important in kitchen/dining rooms that the tableware will look as good on a table set for dinner as on the kitchen countertop. So the simpler the style, the better, but with a hint of elegance. There are variations here, of course. If your kitchen

is a designer one, with lots of expensive stone and stainless steel, match that decorative mood with white bone-china cups in tapered cone shapes, stainless-steel flatware styled with a twist, and plain glasses, but in crystal. If the kitchen is simpler, look for white earthenware plates, teak bowls, and chunky glasses. Luxury is as much about quantity as anything else, so make sure there is a good stock of everything.

Understated luxury is wonderful, but in the same way that a perfectly composed outfit needs a little "messing up," so, too, will a streamlined kitchen. Have fun doing this. It doesn't necessarily involve shopping for new accessories: sometimes, in a very modern setting, the addition of something unexpected such as a stove-top kettle or sherbet-yellow dishtowels will provide enough of an element of surprise.

kitchen
wish list

Walk-in refrigerator/freezer

Catering-style range

Butcher's block preparation table; trolley *(oak, birch counters; stainless steel)*

Benches, chairs, or stools; contemporary or traditional *(solid wood, stainless steel, high-specification plastics)*

Kitchen/dining table, contemporary or traditional *(glass, stainless steel, wood, laminate)*

Ice-cream maker, coffee grinder, bread or yogurt maker

Design classics: blender, mixer, toaster, espresso maker *(chrome, stainless steel, fashion colors)*

Fish steamer, asparagus steamer, pasta maker

Paella, omelet, and blini pans

Chopping board/pastry board *(beech, maple, marble)*

Blowtorch, waffle iron

Electronic salt and pepper mill

bedrooms

Bedrooms need barely more than a bed, storage, and good lighting to become the tranquil retreats most of us crave. So edit choices, keeping that ambience in mind. Of course, the comfort of the basics matter (the mattress, the pillows), but soft textures, purity of line, and the odd splash of indulgence count, too.

bedroom basics

It's a salutary thought that we spend around one third of our lives asleep. Use that fact to help you concentrate on what is important in the bedroom, and to plan the room from the inside out. While it's great to close your eyes on a beautifully designed room full of lovely things, what really counts is what cocoons you as you sleep. Anyone who has ever slept on a top-quality mattress beneath natural bedding will know the true meaning of a good night's sleep.

So put decorative style on the back burner, and instead asterisk a great mattress and good-quality bedding on your real lists. The most comfortable and enduring mattress type is hand-nested and pocket sprung. The next best thing is an open-coil mattress—save thin foam versions for overnight guests. If your mattress is sound, but stained, get it re-upholstered in traditional ticking. Always use a mattress protector to guard against spills and to provide a cushioning layer. Pillows and comforters look neater with protectors, too.

There are other practicalities to consider. Don't automatically buy a mattress for the size of bed frame you have now, if in five years' time you hope to get a more luxuriously proportioned bed. Do you

have young children who join you in the morning (or at night), and if so, would a larger mattress make everyone more comfortable? Do you really need an orthopedic mattress? (Many of us buy them unnecessarily; a medium-firm mattress should offer adequate support.) Good mattress companies will custom-make sizes to accommodate tall people or to fit a non-standard bed frame. Just remember that you won't be able to use standard-size fitted sheets.

Be ruthless, too, when reassessing your existing bedding. For the sake of nightly comfort, budget for some new good-quality basics. Think about quantities. Allow yourself several pillows, plus spares for overnight guests. When buying duvets, consider practical issues. Do you want the type that can be machine-washed at home, or do you and your partner need a design with two different tog ratings? Central heating may mean that a medium-weight duvet (9 tog) or a lightweight summer one (4.5 tog) is warm enough, but in colder areas you might need a winter version (13.5 or 15 tog) as well. A spare double duvet is always helpful for overnight guests and single sizes are the best choice for kids. The best fillings are goose or duck

This page In the same way that plain white bed linen creates that essential neutral basis for the bed, white window dressings perform a similar function. Invest in plain white black-out window shades, or natural pinoleum, and a metal or wood curtain pole, and you can then change the curtains—switching from white voile to embroidered silk—with ease. *Opposite page, inset* Provided there's room for a drink, a wall-mounted or pull-out shelf on the bed frame suffices as a bedside table. Other simple options, adaptable in future years, might include secondhand or ready-to-paint tables with a shelf or drawer, or open-sided rattan cubes.

This page A fresher and more flexible alternative to full sets of matching bed linen, which can be overpowering, is the concept of layering geometric, floral, or striped pillowcases and a flat sheet, with a white comforter or bedcover. *Opposite page* Not everyone wants pure white bed linen all the time. More practical options might include neutrals, from off-white and natural shades through to charcoal or soft gray-blue. If you enjoy splashes of color, buy one or two sets of colored sheets—from pastels to brights—either a matching set or single pieces in a variety of shades. This is a great way to bring a fashion element into the bedroom without vast expense.

down (softer than feathers since there is no quill); but feather fillings are fine. Allergy sufferers should choose hollow-fiber polyester versions, which aren't any less expensive than natural versions.

Your basic white cotton bedlinen should play the same role as white T-shirts: easy to mix with other patterns, timeless, and fresh-looking. Whether buying new or using what you have, make sure you have three sets, and double the pillowcases if you like two pillows. Think about sheets. Life is too short for making beds with hospital corners, so fitted bottom sheets are fine, but do include flat sheets in your basics kit. Not only are they great alone in summer, but they look pretty over a wool blanket or eiderdown. Look for styles with drawn threadwork or embroidery on the top edge.

White bed linen doesn't mean an austere look, since there are so many textural variations. The most enduring, classic styles include double or triple cording, a drawn threadwork edge, or white-on-white embroidery. Then there are chic contemporary variations, from pin-tucks and waffle textures to self-stripes or bold embroidery. Stick to 100 percent cotton, which washes well, but if softness is a priority, consider piqué, cotton jersey, or seersucker. If all-white seems too clinical, consider neutrals such as cream or stone.

Just as neutral upholstery provides the canvas for brighter scatter cushions in a living room, white sheets mean you can play around with fashionable impulse buys and revive wool blankets or that faded chintz eiderdown you already had, which will look fresh and new against an all-white background. While you want to avoid coordinated sets of bedding, which will dominate a room and tie it down to a single look, it's fun to build up an additional wardrobe of bedlinen in bright colors, unusual textures, or funky patterns. There's no great expense involved—simply look out for sale bargains such as bedding sets in last season's hot color.

Now is also the time to reassess bedroom furniture. If you're unhappy with an outmoded bed frame, it's better to get rid of it now, so it doesn't interfere with your other bedroom building-block choices. Then save for the bed of a lifetime. In the short term, there are various options. When buying a new mattress, invest in a studio base to which you can add a luxurious padded or wood-veneer

It's fun to build up a wardrobe of bedlinen in bright colors, unusual textures, or funky patterns.

This page and opposite Often the most tranquil bedrooms are the simplest ones, those filled with little more than a bed, lamp, and somewhere to hang clothes. Make a stylistic virtue out of this fact. Choose utility or rustic-style furnishings that are not only inexpensive, but also provide the only quirky "dressing-up" element a simple bedroom needs. This bed *(below)*, for example, is made from scaffolding tubes. In keeping with the simple style, basics to add to your white bed linen might include hand-knitted pure wool or cotton-waffle blankets, or pastel chambray, gingham, and ticking-stripe bed linens. To complete the mood, make sure the mattress is upholstered in traditional ticking.

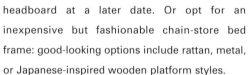

headboard at a later date. Or opt for an inexpensive but fashionable chain-store bed frame: good-looking options include rattan, metal, or Japanese-inspired wooden platform styles.

Your other bedroom basic is clothes storage. Armoires and chests of drawers are classic investment pieces, so may be worth saving for, rather than buying mid-range reproduction furniture that won't look as good in ten years' time. Before making any decisions, take a long hard look at what's in the bedroom; would a good clothes clear-out alter your need for additional storage? If you want furniture now, look for quirky chests of drawers and an armoire that won't cost a fortune, and which can be upgraded with antique

pieces later on. Alternatively, capitalize on utility style and opt for clothes folded and hung on open shelves and hooks or tubular steel hanging rails.

Sift through the remaining basics and figure out what is most important for you, then add them gradually. While everyone will need a good bedside lamp—a gooseneck style is a long-lasting, classic choice—some won't be able to live without a full-length mirror. Others will consider a bedside table a necessity. Don't worry at this stage about other decorative touches. There's a tantalizing simplicity about a pared-down bedroom. As long as there's a table top for a glass vase with fresh flowers, and room for the alarm clock and radio, enjoy that visual peace.

This page and opposite
If funds for a bed are limited, it's a good idea to make do with a classic studio bed and think about a headboard later. Look for a base with useful drawers, then a chest of drawers or extra storage in the bedroom is less of an immediate necessity. Alternatively, build a composite headboard or bed frame. The beauty of a tailormade headboard is that storage such as shelves or drawers can easily be incorporated. An easy alternative is a Japanese sleeping platform furnished with tatami mats.

bedroom
real list

Bedstead *(rattan, wood, iron)*

Mattress, ticking upholstered *(pocket sprung or open coil)*

Chair, upright; upholstered armchair *(wood, metal; white/neutral cotton)*

Armoire, closet *(wood, toughened-glass paneled; tubular steel)*

Bedside tables *(painted board, wood, rattan)*

Lamps *(metal gooseneck style or ceramic with paper shade)*

Pillows, rectangular

Duvet *(goose or duck down, or synthetic fillings)*

Cotton sheets, pillowcases, duvet covers *(white, neutrals, pastels, chambray)*

Blanket *(cellular cotton, fleece, pure new wool)*

Bedspread *(cotton, cotton waffle, plain quilted)*

Clock, radio

This page and opposite page, left The simpler the bedroom, the easier it is to indulge in new looks using eccentric or simply unusual accessories. In this room, the inclusion of three understated, if quirky, pieces—the wall-mounted horns, antique chair, and bamboo table—instantly evokes a neo-colonial mood. Swap these pieces with a framed watercolor, linen slipcovered armchair, and marble-topped side table, and the style would change entirely.

bedroom luxuries

For many, the bedroom is the one space where they feel they can indulge in a little visual (and sensual) splendor. That's perfectly justifiable. The bedroom is a private zone, not a heavy traffic area, so floor coverings, window hangings, and upholstery can be a little more frivolous. Whether you opt for a pure and simple room with subtle luxuries, or full-on boudoir glamour, don't feel guilty about small indulgences. The bedroom is the equivalent of "me time," a place for relaxing.

Invest in a great bed as soon as you can afford to because, inevitably, it is the main decorative focus in the room. A really beautiful bed frame should be a choice for life, one of a handful of pieces of furniture around which your home will evolve over the years. Therefore it is crucial to buy a design you love that won't go out of fashion and which will age well. Before you even start to look in stores or antique markets, look for bedrooms you admire in books or magazines. However modern the rest of the room, it's likely that the bed will be an antique or upholstered style. Unless you are very committed to modern design, there's something rather hard about trendy minimal beds. The watchwords in a bedroom should be comfort, classicism, and serenity.

Above right **Provided it is introduced into a room composed of all the right neutral basics, there is enormous decorative power to be had from the addition of just one luxurious fabric. Team a length of precious antique fabric with a half corona and you get a period look; toss a contemporary fashion colored-silk quilt on to a bed, and the look is different again.**

This page and opposite
If you want delicious glamour in
the bedroom, go ahead and indulge
yourself, but make sure it's possible
to tone down the major features
in years to come. This bedroom
perfectly demonstrates such
flexibility. The silk dress curtains
and bedcover are easily replaced
with something more restrained;
the faux-fur stool cover is tossed
over the stool rather than attached
to it, allowing for a more tailored
slipcover option at a later date.
The mix of decorative styles—
contemporary light fixtures teamed
with a crystal chandelier, ornate
mirror, and cuboid headboard—
also allows the room to be taken
further in either stylistic direction
in the future.

There are certain bed styles that have universal appeal and always look pretty. These range from caned or carved and painted Louis XV-style headboards through to wood or metal Napoleon *bateaux lits*, simple metal campaign beds with swooping curves, Shaker-style wood four-posters, iron bedsteads, and carved colonial-style beds. Try to buy an authentic antique or an old version of a certain period style rather than a reproduction. The patina of the wood or gently faded paintwork is more attractive, and old beds are often less expensive than new ones. Don't be concerned that an antique style will tie a bedroom down to a period look. Upholstered headboards can look modern with plain linens and tickings; while cane and wood are fresh and timeless with white bed linen. Certain woods are too heavy, so try to pick mid-toned woods such as maple, cherry, and oak.

Your choice of bed will be influenced as much by lifestyle as by design preferences. If you like reading in bed, a comfortable upholstered headboard is the best option. Upholstered headboards aren't expensive, so there won't be a major problem updating the current high, rectangular silhouette to something softer as fashions change. An upholstered headboard offers all sorts of options for adding touchy-feely luxury. Leather, nubuck, or velvet are great choices. If you have kids, a removable washable or dry-cleanable cover is better. Stick to neutral tones, as always; or try chocolate, deep purple, or charcoal for a great contrast to white bedding.

Not everyone wants to commit long-term to a single style. If this is the case, choose a design with fabric hangings that will allow you to alter the look from year to year. A simple wooden or metal four-poster can be hung with voile panels, linen curtains, or colorful taffeta. Likewise, a half-corona may be hung with a variety of textiles over the years, transforming an otherwise plain studio base. By keeping the major elements in the rest of the room plain, you have the freedom to indulge in one eye-catching patterned fabric, from antique toile de Jouy to floral chintz. One pattern is fine; too many coordinating fabrics will date.

Historically, luxurious bed linen, from pure linen to monogrammed sheets, was a way to convey an individual's wealth and stature. These days, great quality is more about personal pleasure. If you have the finances, upgrade from white cotton to Irish linen or high-thread-count Egyptian cotton; no one else will notice the difference, but you will enjoy the sensual benefits. For a luxurious look on the bed itself, go for damask-print sateen sheets, embroidery, or lace edging in small quantities. The ultimate is satin, silk, or crêpe-de-chine bed linen. Some can be washed, others must be dry-cleaned; ask yourself how convenient the latter will be?

Alternatively, white cotton sheets can be given a sophisticated new look (and sensuous feel) by teaming them with the wealth of boudoir-chic accessories currently available. Think of blankets,

This page and opposite The most restrained and tailored of bedrooms can still bask in luxurious additions. If this is your chance to invest in a new bed frame or headboard, indulge in either an upholstered version—try leather or suede—or a beautiful wooden model. If your bed is very pared down, dress up the room with unusual bedside tables and/or lamp options. Curvy silhouettes or opulent textures will relieve any sense of austerity.

This page and opposite
For those in search of subtle, understated luxury, look to textures, rather than colors and shapes, to upgrade a room and make it truly wonderful. In an enclosed space such as this room, the impact will be even greater. In a feminine bedroom, curtains are essential, but try to stick to "dress" curtains, teamed with a plain shade, to give maximum flexibility. Luxurious curtain options include satin, silk, taffeta, or silk voile; look out, too, for high-tech modern fabrics featuring pleats or metallic threads. Understated bedcover options might include sheepskins, faux fur, deep-quilted continental matelasse, or a white-on-white embroidered bedspread. When the emphasis is on deep shades and sensuous textures, it's important to be able to swap these for lighter alternatives in summer. This room would look equally pretty and fresh with white linen sheets, and unadorned wooden Venetian blinds.

from alpaca, cashmere, and mohair to cable-knit lambswool and pure new wool. Then there are faux-fur covers or sheepskin throws. Bedspread options include heavy chenille or light-as-a-feather silk organza. For ultimate glamour, there are quilted satin throws and eiderdowns. None of this comes cheap, of course, though inexpensive chain-store copies are increasing. The crucial point is that just one of these items will transform a room.

After the bed, clothes storage should be next on the agenda. Sometimes, it is better to create built-in closets, tailormade to your requirements, and buy a really pretty dressing table than invest in a

For many, the bedroom is the one room in the house where they can justify a little visual splendor.

great-looking armoire that never quite provides all the space you need. Make sure you like a freestanding piece before buying. They can be heavy-looking and crowd a bedroom. A light-wood Shaker-style or painted armoire are usually more attractive choices.

Now is the time to treat yourself to furniture that adds comfort but isn't a necessity. Look at what's on your wish list and check that it's compatible with your lifestyle. If children congregate in your bedroom, a small sofa is more sociable than an armchair. If you read in bed, a bedside table with space for books and magazines will be a priority. The more frivolous the piece, the more fun there is to be had choosing unusual designs. A mirrored Thirties dressing table or elaborate gilt-framed mirror will provide enticing variety.

Exercise restraint when adding luxurious touches to the bedroom, so that the initial flexibility of the basic building blocks remains intact. The neutral base, filled out with classic buys, is always the starting point. But what you have now is a "wardrobe" of pretty extras that can be mixed and matched to create different looks and reflect trends. But be selective, so that the room, however glamorous, retains a certain precious tranquility.

bedroom
wish list

Bed, contemporary designer; antique; upholstered *(wood, metal, cane, fabric)*

Upholstered headboard for divan *(suede, nubuck, leather)*

Bedside tables; decorative or contemporary designer *(marble-topped, solid wood or veneer)*

Mirror; antique or modern *(gilded, Venetian, wood surround)*

Dressing table; antique or contemporary *(mirror finish, solid wood or veneer)*

Armchair, small sofa, daybed; upholstered *(linen, silk, wool)*

Chandelier; silk-shaded lamps

Rug *(sheepskin, antique, pure new wool)*

Sheets, pillowcases, duvet covers *(silk, satin, linen)*

Throws *(faux fur, wool, satin, velvet)*

Bedspreads or quilts *(chenille, silk, satin, matelasse)*

Scatter cushions *(satin and linen, knitted leather, ponyskin)*

Vases, candles, photo frames, trinket boxes

bathrooms

However simple its design, every bathroom should offer soft towels, a mat underfoot, and somewhere to store toiletries. It's your choice whether the bathroom is a place to linger, or a get-up-and-go washroom; choose the accessories to suit. Divide the emphasis squarely between durability and good looks, and your choices will endure.

bathroom basics

Many people consider it a luxury to install a bathroom from scratch. More likely, they will make do with a previous owner's choices, adapting what is already there. But think carefully about this while assessing your home. Every other room in the house is the sum of the pieces you put into it, but the bathroom is dominated by its sanitary-ware. If you don't like the style or color, then no amount of careful choosing and editing of accessories will alter the look. So, a new bathroom may rise to the top of your real, or wish, list. Think of it another way. The sofa is the major "classic" investment in the living room. Plainly styled white sanitaryware is the equivalent in the bathroom. It will always be worth the investment, because it can be dressed with so many different looks.

If the existing appliances are white, but old-fashioned, much can be done by effecting small changes. Faucets may seem insignificant, but can make a radical impact on a room. Try replacing old ones with sleek contemporary versions. They needn't be expensive designer lines—the choice of modern, budget faucets is ever-widening. The basin is also a tool for making a strong style statement. Swapping a traditional pedestal variety for a modern bowl set into a storage unit creates an entirely new look. A change in bath siding, from painted board to toughened sandblasted glass, is another option. Or the judicious inclusion of a reconditioned salvage piece (a ceramic sink or quirky old-fashioned faucets) can add a pretty, decorative twist to a plain bathroom.

This page **If you're sufficiently committed to a color to choose all-over mosaic tiles, then rule number one is to keep all other accessories neutral. This still offers plenty of choice: everything from hard shiny finishes such as stainless steel to bumpy sisal weaves and rough-hewn stone.**

Opposite page **In contrast, the all-white bathroom provides a neutral basis for adding color. One year, the room might be accessorized with hot-pink towels; the next, a restrained combination of natural textures. The all-white bathroom is an excellent choice for kids, who inevitably have less tasteful and more colorful accessories on show.**

This page Even the most tasteful of individuals can fall foul of novelty shower curtains, toilet seats, and toothbrush holders, often emblazoned with everything from glitter to bobbing yellow ducks, and purchased in the sincere belief they will sharpen up a plain and understated bathroom. Be warned—they won't. It's far better to stick to clear plastic and/or glass and use bright blocks of color to inject a splash of individuality.

Opposite page Just because you've opted for a supremely pared-down bathroom doesn't mean that all accessories need to be utilitarian. There's a huge choice of attractive storage jars, soap dishes, boxes, and toothbrush holders available in every conceivable finish and material, from mother-of-pearl and soapstone to granite or punched metalwork. These are your "dress-up" indulgences. Make a promise to update them each year.

The towel rod is a crucial basic. If the bathroom is being installed from scratch, choose a heated model. Some may consider this a luxury, but it's the best basic you can invest in. Match your towel rod to your lifestyle. In a family bathroom, a multi-rail is essential, while smaller numbers of towels look good on ring holders. A bamboo ladder gives a more eclectic look and won't date.

A mirror and chair or stool are also essentials, even in a tiny bathroom. Avoid frosted-glass or pattern-emblazoned mirrors or cork-topped stools, which will either date or simply lack character. Instead, choose a mix of simple pieces that can blend with any style of sanitaryware. Ultra-plain is fine—a round glass mirror or slatted-wood folding chair will last forever—or seek out unusual pieces that will inject a little individuality.

When choosing storage, it's tempting to be swept away by the sort of open glass shelves or colored acrylic drawer-trolleys specially designed for bathrooms. Try, instead, to pick storage in natural, neutral-colored materials and in a style that appeals to you. If you can imagine the piece still looking good in another room, you're on the right track. Woven seagrass baskets and lidded trunks; a freestanding, retro-style metal cabinet; or a stainless-steel trolley are all possibilities. Alternatively, the traditional metal or glass-fronted medicine cabinet is the ultimate classic.

Don't forget small but important basics such as the toilet brush, toilet seat, and toothbrush holder. How they look (and function) really does matter, since they are used every day. Pick the simplest designs in good-quality natural materials, from a stainless-steel toilet brush to a soapstone soap dish. Manufacturers fall over themselves in an

attempt to brighten these items with fussy detail or novelty colors. Resist! Tasteless accessories can ruin a pared-down bathroom.

Yet, unless you want a particularly austere bathroom, a splash of well-edited color and a dash of frivolity is essential. Once you have the neutral building blocks in place, concentrate on finding pretty or fashionable accessories that will bring the bathroom to life. Your toothbrush holder doesn't have to be a traditional glass-and-chrome affair—it could be a Turkish tea glass, a lime-green child's beaker, or a quirky pottery cup. For storage jars, investigate not just the bathroom options, but also kitchen jars, from glass to stainless steel, ethnic baskets, or secondhand finds. The bathmat is another vehicle for introducing a splash of color:

look out for bright rubber or photo-print plastic designs. All these things are fun and fashionable, yet easy to change in a year's time.

White towels are always the best buy, not only because they look fresh and will go with every tile or wall color, but also because they won't fade, as many bright colors do after years of washing. In terms of practicality, when buying new, invest in a small hand towel and give it a few washes to test for absorbency and softness. Try to buy the best quality—good towels should last at least ten years. Look carefully at sizes. Although jumbo bath towels seem tempting, they can be too large to squeeze on to a towel rod. For interest, look out for variations on white such as ribbed or waffle textures or stone, charcoal, and black colorways.

White towels are always the best buy, not only because they look fresh and will go with every tile or wall color, but also because they won't fade as bright colors do.

Opposite page, below left The beauty of planning an austere, plain bathroom, is that, like the combination of white shirt and blue jeans, it becomes the basic canvas for endless "dress up" variations. The retro chair and ethnic baskets in this bathroom make a fabulous contrast; but so, too, would a vivid scarlet contemporary stool.

Opposite page, below right There is a satisfying tranquility about visually and practically editing a room down to the absolute basics. Don't spoil it with patterned toiletry packaging; decant bath oils into plain glass bottles and jars.

This page and inset Not everyone wants a bare bathroom. Have fun introducing quirky buys to bring individuality to the basic sanitaryware. Think laterally around the subject. In this bathroom, medicines are stored in a cast-iron box rather than a traditional wall-mounted cabinet.

bathroom
real list

Bathroom cabinet *(stainless steel, glass-fronted, wood)*

Stool/chair; secondhand or classic *(wood, metal, plastic)*

Towel rod; built-in or freestanding *(chrome, stainless steel, wood, bamboo)*

Mirror *(plain, stainless steel, or wood surround)*

Laundry basket *(rattan, muslin-lined wood)*

Storage unit/shelving *(rattan; wood, metal)*

Bathroom scales

Towels; bath and hand sizes
*(plain, ribbed, waffle; white
or neutral)*

Bathmat
(terrycloth, cork, wood)

**Toilet-paper holder and
brush** *(metal, plastic, wood)*

Storage jars and boxes
(seagrass, glass, metal, stone)

Soap dish, toothbrush glass
(ceramic, stone, glass, metal)

Shower curtain
(clear or colored plastic)

bathroom luxuries

The notion of luxury in the bathroom is particularly subjective, because we all use this room in different ways. For those who like to get up and go, a no-nonsense wet room is the ultimate luxury; for loungers, a big tub and somewhere to put a drink is essential. Look at your wish lists; what do you really crave? If it's a power shower, the investment involved in converting a mediocre bathroom into a huge shower room is worthwhile. Certain other luxuries are only possible if you can start from scratch. These include inset ceiling speakers, for music in the bathroom, underfloor heating, and pump-assisted plumbing for excellent water pressure.

If finances permit, you might choose to include just one amazing new piece of sanitaryware that is not only sensually pleasing, but will look cutting edge (and these days, bathrooms hold equal ratings with kitchens for being a designer statement). This might be something as radical as replacing your tub with a wooden Japanese one or an oval stainless-steel version. Alternatively, an ordinary wall-mounted acrylic sink may be

Opposite page **Just as a leather jacket looks best teamed with a simple white shirt, rather than one that's elaborately patterned, so richly finished surfaces need similar treatment. In this elegant marbled bathroom, accessories have been restricted to pure white towels and little else.**
Above left **It's fun to experiment with the odd ornate piece. In a** bathroom intended as much for lounging as washing, the inclusion of gilded mirrors, silk lampshades, or paintings not only upgrades the mood, but individualizes the anonymous white sanitaryware.
Above **A bathroom can look pared down, yet still be the best place to relax. Sometimes, a decent-sized tub, central faucets, and flickering candles are all that's required.**

replaced with a toughened glass, stone, or stainless-steel bowl on a pedestal. Sleek designer faucets or minimal spouts can also be added to simple white appliances.

Those satisfied with the basic look, but who want a more polished look and sophisticated mood, should pay attention to the finishes in the bathroom, notably the bathtub or vanity-unit paneling and countertops. The obvious choices are stone, from limestone and granite to marble or concrete, or water-resistant hardwoods such as teak, mahogany, or iroko. None of these come cheap: a slab of marble can cost as much as a sofa. Yet it is amazing how the inclusion of even a small piece of stone or wood can upgrade a bathroom. Remember to think of it as "furniture" for the bathroom. Get the surfaces right, and a bathroom can look so cool and sophisticated that accessories can be kept to the monastic minimum.

Good lighting is essential in a bathroom; it must work efficiently by day and night to provide task illumination for shaving and be adjustable to create the correct level for relaxation. If you are starting from scratch, the most luxurious

Below left Many of us prefer showers, but they don't have to be clinical and functional. Good-looking natural surfaces, including stone or concrete, a powerful pump and generous shower space (as well as somewhere to sit) can provide plenty of sensual luxury.
Below right The addition of only one quality surface—here, a solid limestone wash basin—can lift an otherwise plain and simple bathroom, with its ordinary mirror and sleek spout, to decorative, and sensual, new heights.

combination of lighting includes low-voltage ceiling lights on a dimmer switch with side lights flanking the mirror to cast a flattering and helpful light for make-up. But it's not always possible to alter bathroom lighting (though you shouldn't overlook candlelight as a great mood-maker at night). If that's the case, concentrate on achieving good light control during the day. This means investing in a flexible window treatment that provides privacy but lets in maximum daylight. The best investment will be a set of plantation shutters or wooden Venetian blinds.

For some, luxury is not so much about sensual comfort as extreme efficiency. A quality mirror comes top of the list. If the bathroom doubles as a dressing room, get a full-length mirror (ideally, one that pivots); if shaving or making up is a priority, invest in one on a flexible arm. Other good choices include mirrors that come with an electric heating pad behind (to prevent steaming up), and those with built-in lighting. For organized individuals who like accessible storage, built-in cabinets and drawers installed beneath a vanity counter top will be the ultimate.

Below left and right **When a bathroom is shared by both sexes, it takes plenty of careful thought to make sure that differing preferences and dual notions of luxury are met. This room caters amply to both needs. The large round and magnifying mirrors, perfect for shaving, are conveniently situated next to the washbasin, while the make-up-height mirror, close to a source of natural light and attached to a custommade jewelry and toiletries stand, has been planned with the woman in mind.**

Left and below left This bathroom demonstrates perfectly how to update stylishly an existing bathroom. Victorian-style cast iron legs were boarded in, creating a contemporary shape, old-fashioned faucets were swapped for sleek designer ones, and the entire tub was painted off-white. Think of this exercise as the equivalent of having a suit altered to get an up-to-date new silhouette.

Opposite page The nice thing about a plain white bathroom is that it can be positively chameleonlike, depending on the other pieces you add to the room. This large-scaled verre eglomise mirror panel has transformed a family bathroom into a glamorous relaxation zone.

The truly relaxing bathroom is something of a comfort zone. Try to think of the bathroom not as a clinical washroom, but like any other room in the house. If space permits, a small sofa is a great idea—keep upholstery neutral and splash-resistant, such as soft terrycloth. Alternatively, a dresser or chest of drawers could be added.

It can feel very luxurious to add unexpected fabrics and textures to the bathroom. Clipping an antique linen sheet in front of a plastic shower curtain or white window shades is one option; laying a rug on the floor is another. It's your choice whether these extras are colorful or neutral—a splash of color can be uplifting in a pared-down space.

> *Try to think of the bathroom not just as a clinical washroom, but like any other room in the house. If space permits, a small sofa is a great idea.*

If you are already armed with white towels, invest in some extras to provide the luxury of choice. A set of towels in a color you love can offset the severity of stone surfaces. Monogrammed towels or embroidered guest towels trimmed with satin ribbon are a true luxury. Exercise great restraint when choosing accessories. If there are polished stone or wood surfaces, contrast that glamour with glass canisters and boxes. Sleek white appliances could be pepped up with a metal bowl of scented soaps. Don't forget the power of paintings. Provided the bathroom is well ventilated, art won't suffer and provides the perfect individual stamp for creating a relaxing, private room.

bathroom *wish list*

Designer bowl/wash basin *(glass, stone, steel)*

Contemporary faucets/spouts

Armchair; upholstered stool *(rattan; terrycloth or cotton)*

Window shades *(linen, wood Venetian, plantation shutters)*

Towels, decorative *(colored; linen-edged, waffle, linen)*

Guest towels *(monogrammed or hemstitched linen, embroidered, ribbon-trimmed)*

Containers and jars *(glass, gilded, stone, metal)*

Glass bath or perfume bottles *(etched, colored, gilded)*

Full-length mirror *(plain wood or metal, gilded, carved)*

Magnifying shaving/make-up mirror

Scented candles, incense holders

Laundry basket *(punched stainless steel, steamed wood)*

suppliers

CLASSICS

Laura Ashley Home Store
171 East Ridgewood Avenue
Ridgewood, NJ 07450
201-670-0686
www.laura-ashleyusa.com
Floral, striped, checked, and solid cotton
fabrics in a wide variety of colors.

Ruby Beets Antiques
Poxybogue Road
Bridgehampton, NY 11932
516-537-2802
Painted furniture and kitchenware.

Crate & Barrel
646 N Michigan Avenue
Chicago, IL 60611
800-996-9960
www.crateandbarrel.com
Good-value furniture and accessories,
from simple white china and glass to
chairs and beds.

Design Within Reach
455 Jackson Street
San Francisco, CA 94111
800-944-2233
www.dwr.com
Contemporary designer furniture.

English Country Antiques
Snake Hollow Road
Bridgehampton, NY 11932
516-537-0606
Period country furniture.

Full Upright Position
800-431-5134
www.fup.com
Furniture designed by Aalto, Eames,
Le Corbusier, van der Rohe and more.

Kohler
Locations throughout U.S.
800-456-4537
www.kohlerco.com
Furniture, plumbing, and artist edition
sinks for the modern kitchen.

On Board Fabrics
Route 27
P.O. Box 14
Edgecomb, ME 04556
207-882-7536
www.onboardfabrics.com
Everything from plain cottons to Italian
tapestry and woven plaids.

Palecek
The Design Pavilion #27
200 Kansas Street
San Francisco, CA 94103
800-274-7730
www.palecek.com
Painted wicker furniture and
accessories with a exotic feel.

Pottery Barn
600 Broadway
New York, NY 10012
800-922-5507
www.potterybarn.com
Good-quality furniture and decorative
accessories.

Smith + Noble
Corona, CA
800-560-0027
www.smithandnoble.com
Custommade window treatments, rugs,
pillows, slipcovers, and duvet covers.

Williams-Sonoma
121 East 59th Street
New York, NY 10022
800-541-1262
www.williams-sonomainc.com
Cooking utensils, fine linens, and
classic china.

Workbench
470 Park Avenue South
New York, NY 10016
800-380-2370
www.workbenchfurniture.com
Clean and functional Danish furniture
for bedrooms, eating and living rooms.

BASICS

Bed, Bath & Beyond
620 Avenue of the Americas
New York, NY 10011
212-255-3550
www.bedbathandbeyond.com
Everything for the bedroom and
bathroom, plus kitchen utensils, home
décor, and storage solutions.

Fishs Eddy
889 Broadway
New York, NY 10011
212-420-2090
Overstock supplies of simple Fifties-
style china mugs, plates, bowls, etc.

Hancock Fabrics
2605A West Main Street
Tupelo, MS 38801
662-844-7368
www.hancockfabrics.com
America's largest fabric store, good for
all basic decoration needs.

Hold Everything
1309–1311 Second Avenue
New York, NY 10021
212-879-1450
www.williams-sonomainc.com
Everything for storage, from baskets to
bookshelves.

IKEA
1800 East Mc Connor Parkway
Schaumburg, IL 60173
www.ikea.com
Simple, well-designed assembly kit
furniture and inexpensive kitchenware.

Janovic
1150 Third Avenue
New York, NY 10021
800-772-4381
www.janovic.com
Quality paints in a wide color range.

Jennifer Convertibles
3302/3304 M Street NW
Washington, DC 20007
202-333-0080
www.jenniferfurniture.com
Sleeper sofas, rugs, and sheets.

Restoration Hardware
935 Broadway
New York, NY 10011
212-260-9479
www.restorationhardware.com
Not just hardware, but home
furnishings, lighting and accessories.

**Martha Stewart Paint Collection
At Kmart**
888-627-8429
www.bluelight.com
A quality selection of decorator shades
inspired by Martha's Araucana chickens.

Target
900 Nicollet Mall
Minneapolis, MN 55403
612-338-0085
www.target.com
Home furnishings, bed and bath
supplies, kitchen goods, and more.

Waverly
800-423-5881
www.waverly.com
Fabrics, furniture, window treatments,
accessories, and floor coverings.

LUXURIES

ABC Carpet & Home
881–888 Broadway
New York, NY 10003
212-674-1144
www.abchome.com
Home furnishings, fabrics, carpets, and
design accessories.

B & B Italia USA
150 East 58th Street
New York, NY 10155
800-872-1697
www.bebitalia.it
Furniture by Bellini, Cittero, Pesce,
Scarpa, and others.

Victor DiPaola Antiques
Long Island, NY
516-488-5868
www.dipaolaantiques.com
Furniture and decorative arts of the
18th and 19th centuries.

Michael C. Fina
545 Fifth Avenue
New York, NY 10017
1-800-BUY-FINA
www.michaelcfina.com
Silverware, glassware, and china.

Frette Inc.
799 Madison Avenue
New York, NY 10021
212-988-5221
www.frette.it
Exclusive Italian linens for table, bed, and bath.

Garnet Hill
P.O. Box 262, Main Street
Franconia, NH 03580
www.garnethill.com
Bedlinen in natural fibers, plus wonderful down duvets and pillows.

Gump's
135 Post Street
San Francisco, CA 94108
800-882-8055 or 415-982-1616
www.gumps.com
A full selection of luxury home items, including garden and patio furniture.

Calvin Klein Home
At Calvin Klein
645 Madison Avenue
New York, NY 10021
212-292-9000
Classic linens and blankets.

Ralph Lauren Paint Collection
At Ralph Lauren
867 Madison Avenue
New York, NY 10021
212-606-2100
Signature collection of paint colors grouped in themes.

Missoni Home
At Missoni
1009 Madison Avenue
New York, NY 10021
212-517-9339
Boutique with modern fabric designs.

Poggenpohl
145 U.S. Hwy 46W, Suite 200
Wayne, NJ 07470
800-987-0553
www.poggenpohl-usa.com
Customized kitchen design.

Portico Bed & Bath
139 Spring Street
New York, NY 10012
212-941-7800
White linens, towels and throws.

Takashimaya
693 Fifth Avenue
New York, NY 10012
212-350-0100
Exclusive bedlinen, soaps, and lotions as well as scented candles and other luxurious accessories.

Waterworks
23 West Putnam Avenue
Greenwich, CT 06830
800-998-BATH or 203-869-7766
www.waterworks.com
Bathroom fixtures, furniture, lighting, and fittings.

Williamsburg Marketplace Catalogue
The Colonial Williamsburg Foundation
Department 023
P.O. Box 3532
Williamsburg, VA 23187
800-414-6291
www.williamsburgmarketplace.com
A selection of historically accurate home furnishings, prints, and other accessories.

DRESSING UP

Anthropologie
1700 Sansom Street, 6th Floor
Philadelphia, PA 19103
800-309-2500
www.anthropologie.com
Funky, one-of-a-kind furniture, accessories, hardware, bedding, rugs, and drapes.

Brimfield Antique Show
Route 20
Brimfield, MA 01010
413-245-3436
www.brimfieldshow.com
This show is held for a week in the months of May, July, and September. For listings of flea markets held throughout the country, go to www.fleamarketguide.com.

Fabrics To Dye For
Two River Road
Pawcatuck, CT 06379
800-322-1319
www.fabricstodyefor.com
Hand-painted fabrics, dyes, and kits.

Ligne Roset
250 Park Avenue
New York, NY 10003
800-BY-ROSET
www.ligne-roset-usa.com
Finely crafted products by original designers with innovative shapes, textures, and materials.

MOMA Design Store
44 West 53rd Street
New York, NY 10022
800-447-6662
www.momastore.org
Furniture, lighting, and accessories by modern designers.

NOVICA
11835 W. Olympic Blvd. Suite 750E
Los Angeles, CA 90064
1-877-2-NOVICA or 310-479-6115
www.novica.com
Unique online store operating in conjunction with National Geographic to provide home décor, furniture, art, and other objects directly from artisans in the Andes, Bali, Java, Brazil, Cuba, India, Mexico, Thailand, and Africa.

Pier One Imports
71 Fifth Avenue
New York, NY 10003
212-206-1911
www.pier1.com
Great home accessories, furniture and outdoor ideas.

Salsa Fabrics
3100 Holly Avenue
Silver Springs, NV 89429
800-758-3819
www.salsafabrics.com
Great original fabrics in cotton, silk, and wool from Guatemala and Indonesia.

Tri-State Antique Center
47 West Pike
Canonsburg, PA 15317
724-745-9116
www.tristateantiques.com
Specializes in Heywood-Wakefield, Mid-Century Modern furniture, and pottery, china, and glass.

Up The Creek's
American Antique Furniture Market
120 South Tower
Centralia, WA 98531
360-330-0427
www.amerantfurn.com
Antique furniture and lighting in Victorian, Eastlake, Turn-of-the-century, Mission, Arts & Crafts, Depression and 1940's Classic Revival periods in both restored and original finish.

Urban Outfitters
Broadway & Bleeker
628 Broadway
New York, NY 10012
212-475-0009
www.urbanoutfitters.com
Trendy tableware, candleholders and accessories.

picture credits

All photography by Jan Baldwin
Key: a = above, b = below, r = right, l = left, c = center

Front & back endpapers: Olivia Douglas & David DiDomenico's apartment in New York, designed by CR Studio Architects, PC; **1** Mona Nerenberg and Lisa Bynon's house in Sag Harbor; **2 & 3** inset Fay Ripley and Daniel Lapaine's apartment in London, designed by Trevyn McDowell and Alastair Galbraith from Site Specific; **4 & 5** Designer Chester Jones' house in London; **6ar** Clare Mosley's house in London; **8-9** Peter & Nicole Dawes' apartment, designed by Mullman Seidman Architects; **10-11** Olivia Douglas & David DiDomenico's apartment in New York, designed by CR Studio Architects, PC ; **11a** a house in New York designed by Brendan Coburn and Joseph Smith from Coburn Architecture; **11b** Jan Hashey and Yasuo Minagawa; **12** Designer Chester Jones' house in London; **13al** Art dealer Gul Coskun's apartment in London; **14al & br** Jan Hashey and Yasuo Minagawa; **14bl** Interior Architect Joseph Dirand's apartment in Paris; **15** Emma Wilson's house in London; **16** Olivia Douglas & David DiDomenico's apartment in New York, designed by CR Studio Architects, PC; **17** Christopher Leach's apartment in London; **18l & 19** Mona Nerenberg and Lisa Bynon's house in Sag Harbor; **20** Constanze von Unruh's house in London; **22 l&r** Interior Architect Joseph Dirand's apartment in Paris; **23** Interior Designer Didier Gomez's apartment in Paris; **24al** Emma Wilson's house in London; **26 & 27r** Fay Ripley and Daniel Lapaine's apartment in London, designed by Trevyn McDowell and Alastair Galbraith from Site Specific; **27l** David Gill's house in London; **28-29c** Jan Hashey and Yasuo Minagawa; **32-33** mosaics designed by Catherine Parkinson; **34** all Designer Chester Jones' house in London; **35l** a house in New York designed by Brendan Coburn and Joseph Smith from Coburn Architecture; **35r** Gabriele Sanders' Long Island home; **37** Jan Hashey and Yasuo Minagawa; **38-39** mosaics designed by Catherine Parkinson; **40** Constanze von Unruh's house in London; **41l** Peter & Nicole Dawes' apartment, designed by Mullman Seidman Architects; **41r** Christopher Leach's apartment in London; **42** all Olivia Douglas & David DiDomenico's apartment in New York, designed by CR Studio Architects, PC; **43** Interior Architect Joseph Dirand's apartment in Paris; **44 & 45ar** Mona Nerenberg and Lisa Bynon's house in Sag Harbor; **45bl &br** Emma Wilson's house in London; **46** furniture made by Sam Miller.; **47** Gabriele Sanders' Long Island home; **48a & 49** Jan Hashey and Yasuo Minagawa; **52 a & b** Art Dealer Gul Coskun's apartment in London; **53** all Designer Chester Jones' house in London; **54 & 55** Interior Designer Didier Gomez's apartment in Paris; **56 & 57l** Constanze von Unruh's house in London; **57r** Christopher Leach's apartment in London; **58-59** all David Gill's house in London; **62** a house in New York designed by Brendan Coburn and Joseph Smith from Coburn Architecture; **65ar** Mona Nerenberg and Lisa Bynon's house in Sag Harbor; **65br** Olivia Douglas & David DiDomenico's apartment in New York, designed by CR Studio Architects, PC; **66-67** all a house in New York designed by Brendan Coburn and Joseph Smith from Coburn Architecture; **68–69** Emma Wilson's house in London; **72** Interior Designer Didier Gomez's apartment in Paris; **73ar** Art Dealer Gul Coskun's apartment in London; **73bl&r** Gabriele Sanders' Long Island home; **74-75c** Christopher Leach's apartment in London; **75r** Clare Mosley's house in London; **76** Jan Hashey and Yasuo Minagawa; **77** Constanze von Unruh's house in London; **80** Jan Hashey and Yasuo Minagawa; **81l** Interior Architect Joseph Dirand's apartment in Paris; **81r** Mona Nerenberg and Lisa Bynon's house in Sag Harbor; **82 l&r** Emma Wilson's house in London; **83** Fay Ripley and Daniel Lapaine's apartment in London, designed by Trevyn McDowell and Alastair Galbraith from Site Specific; **84al** a house in New York designed by Brendan Coburn and Joseph Smith from Coburn Architecture; **84bl, 85** all Architect Joseph Dirand's apartment in Paris; **86-87** mosaics designed by Catherine Parkinson; **90** Constanze von Unruh's house in London; **91** David Gill's house in London; **92-93** Peter & Nicole Dawes' apartment, designed by Mullman Seidman Architects; **94al** Jan Hashey and Yasuo Minagawa; **94bl** Gabriele Sanders' Long Island home; **95** Christopher Leach's apartment in London; **98-99** Interior Designer Didier Gomez's apartment in Paris; **100 & 101** Jan Hashey and Yasuo Minagawa; **100 inset** Olivia Douglas & David DiDomenico's apartment in New York, designed by CR Studio Architects, PC; **102** Peter & Nicole Dawes' apartment, designed by Mullman Seidman Architects; **103** Gabriele Sanders' Long Island home; **104** Emma Wilson's house in London; **106al** Architect Joseph Dirand's apartment in Paris; **106ar** Olivia Douglas & David DiDomenico's apartment in New York, designed by CR Studio Architects, PC; **106bl & 107** a house in New York designed by Brendan Coburn and Joseph Smith from Coburn Architecture; **110 & 111al** Christopher Leach's apartment in London; **111r** Clare Mosley's house in London; **112-113** Fay Ripley and Daniel Lapaine's apartment in London, designed by Trevyn McDowell and Alastair Galbraith from Site Specific; **114** David Gill's house in London; **115** Designer Chester Jones' house in London; **116-117** Art Dealer Gul Coskun's apartment in London; **120** A house in New York designed by Brendan Coburn and Joseph Smith from Coburn Architecture; **121l** Constanze von Unruh's house in London; **121r** Gabriele Sanders' Long Island home; **122** Constanze von Unruh's house in London; **123** Fay Ripley and Daniel Lapaine's apartment in London, designed by Trevyn McDowell and Alastair Galbraith from Site Specific; **124** Olivia Douglas & David DiDomenico's apartment in New York, designed by CR Studio Architects, PC; **125** Peter & Nicole Dawes' apartment, designed by Mullman Seidman Architects; **126** Architect Joseph Dirand's apartment in Paris; **130 & 131l** Christopher Leach's apartment in London; **131r** Interior Designer Didier Gomez's apartment in Paris; **132** David Gill's house in London; **133** both Chester Jones' house in London; **134** Art Dealer Gul Coskun's apartment in London; **135** Clare Mosley's house in London; **143** mosaics designed by Catherine Parkinson.

architects and designers featured in this book

Lisa Bynon Garden Design
P O Box 897
Sag Harbor, NY 11963
t. 631 725 4680.
*Pages 1, 18l, 19, 44, 45 ar, 65 ar,
and 81 r*

Coburn Architecture
70 Washington Street
Studio 1001
Brooklyn, NY 11201
t. 718 875 5052
f. 718 488 8305
email: info@coburnarch.com
www.coburnarch.com
*Pages 11a, 35l, 62, 66-67 all, 84 al,
106 bl, 107, and 120*

Coskun Fine Art London
93 Walton Street
London SW3 2HP
England
t. +44 20 7581 9056
f. +44 20 7581 9056
email: gulgallery@aol.com
www.coskunfineart.com
*Pages 13 al, 52 a & b, 73 ar,
116-117, and 134*

CR Studio Architects, PC
6 West 18th Street, 9th fl.
New York, NY 10011
t. 212 989 8187
f. 212 924 4282
email: victoria@crstudio.com
www.crstudio.com
*Pages 10-11, 16, 42, 65 br, 100
inset, 106 ar, 124, and endpapers*

Dirand Joseph Architecture
338 rue des Pyrenees
75020 Paris
France
t. f. +33 01 47 97 78 57
email: JOSEPH.dirand@wanadoo.fr
*Pages 14 bl, 22 l & r, 43, 81 l, 84 bl,
85 all, 106 al, and 126*

Chester Jones Ltd
Interior Designers
240 Battersea Park Road
London SW11 4NG
England
t. +44 20 7498 2717
f. +44 20 7498 7312
email: chester.jones@virgin.net
*Pages 4, 5, 12, 34 all, 53 all, 115,
and 133*

Christopher Leach Design Ltd
Interior Designer
The Studio
13 Crescent Place
London SW3
England
t. +44 20 7235 2648
f. +44 20 7235 2669
email: mail@christopherleach.com
*Pages 17, 41 r, 57 r, 74-75, 95, 110,
111 al, 130, and 131 l*

Sam Miller
Furniture Maker
t. +44 20 8878 3850
email: sammiller@i12.com
Page 46

Clare Mosley
Gilding, églomisé panels, lamps
t. +44 20 7 708 3123
Pages 6 tr, 75 r, 111 r, and 135

Mullman Seidman Architects
443 Greenwich Street
New York NY 10013
t. 212 431 0770
f. 212 431 8428
email: msa&mullmanseidman.com
*Pages 8, 9, 41 l, 92-93, 102, and
125*

Mona Nerenberg
Bloom
Home and garden products and
antiques
43 Madison Street
Sag Harbor, NY 11963
t. 631 725 4680
*Pages 1, 18l, 19, 44, 45 ar, 65 ar,
and 81 r*

Ory Gomez
Didier Gomez
Interior Designer
15 rue Henri Heine
75016 Paris
France
t. +33 01 44 30 8823
f. +33 01 45 25 1816
email: orygomez@free.fr
*Pages 23, 54, 55, 72, 98, 99, and
131 r*

Catherine Parkinson
Mosaics
t. +44 20 8964 1945
*Pages 32-33, 38-39, 86-87, and
143*

Site Specific
Interior Design & Architecture
60a Peartree Street
London EC1V 35B
England
t. +44 20 7490 3176
f. +44 20 740 3427
email: office@sitespecificltd.co.uk
www.sitespecificltd.co.uk
*Pages 2, 3 inset, 26, 27r, 83,
112-113, and 123*

Constanze von Unruh
Constanze Interior Projects
Interior Design Company
Richmond, Surrey
England
t. +44 20 8948 5533
email: constanze@
constanzeinteriorprojects.com
*Pages 20, 40, 56, 57 l, 77, 90, 121 l,
and 122*

index

**Page numbers in *italics*
refer to captions**

A
accessories, 32–37
    living rooms, 58
armoires, 106, 117

B
basics, 21–24
    bathrooms, 122–129
    bedrooms, 100–109
    eating rooms, 65–71
    kitchens, 83–89
    living rooms, 42–51
bathrooms, 121–37
    basics, 122–129
    color, *123*
    luxuries, 131–137
    mirrors, 124, 133, *135*
    real lists, 128–129
    wish lists, 136–137
bedding, 100–103, 114–117
bedrooms, 99–119
    basics, 100–109
    furniture, *101*, 103–107
    future planning, *112*
    headboards, *107*, 113
    lighting, 106
    luxury, 111–119
    real lists, 108–109
    storage, 106, 117
    textures, *116*
    wish lists, 118–119
beds, 100–106, 111–114
budgets, 13, *24*
buying objects, 21

C
chairs:
    dining areas, 64–77
    living rooms, 52–60
classics, 14–19
closets, 106, 117

color, 19, 24, 27, 30
    bathrooms, *123*, 126
    living rooms, *43*, *44*, 46–48
contemporary designer furniture,
    57

D
defining components, 8–37
dining rooms *see* eating rooms
dressing up, 32–37
    bedrooms, 106
    kitchens, 86
    living rooms, 48

E
eating rooms, 63–79
    basics, 65–71
    lighting, *67*
    luxuries, 73–79
    real list, 70–71
    tableware, 69, 73, 76
    wish lists, 78–79
ethnic styles:
    eating rooms, *64*
    kitchens, *91*
exotic items, living rooms, 58

F
fabric furnishings, *20*
fashion, 17–19
faucets, bathroom, 122, *131*, 132,
    134
finishing touches, 32–37
flamboyant detailing, *58*
focal points, *53*

J
junk shops, 19

K
kitchens, 81–97
    appliances, 84
    basics, 83–89
    dressing up, 86, *87*
    equipment, 83–86, 91–93
    furniture, *83*, *85*, 86, 93–94
    gadgets, 93, *93*
    luxuries, 90–97

open plan, *95*
    real lists, 88–89
    tableware, *91*, 94
    units, *85*
    wish lists, 96–97
    see also eating rooms

L
layered effects, *27*
lighting:
    bathrooms, 132–133
    bedrooms, 106
    eating rooms, *67*
lists, 10–13
living rooms, 41–61
    accessories, 58
    basics, 42–51
    color, *43*, *44*, 46–48
    dressing up, 48
    fail-safe designs, 46
    key pieces, *44*
    luxuries, 52–61
    real list, 50–51
    versatility, 45
    wish list, 60–61
luxuries, 27–30
    bedrooms, 111–119
    eating rooms, 73–79
    kitchen, 90–97
    living rooms, 52–61
    understated luxury, *55*

M
mirrors, bathrooms, 124, 133,
    135

O
ornamentation, 32–37

P
photographs, 14
practicality, 21, *25*

R
real lists, 10–13, *22*
    bathrooms, 128–129
    bedrooms, 108–109
    eating rooms, 70–71

kitchens, 88–89
    living rooms, 50–51
reassessment, 10–13
retro styles, kitchens, *91*
rustic styles:
    bedrooms, *104*
    eating rooms, *64*

S
seating:
    dining areas, 64–77
    kitchens, *83*, 94
    living rooms, 52–60
simplicity, 22
sofas and couches, 42–59
storage:
    bathrooms, 124
    bedrooms, 106, 117
    eating areas, 67–69
suppliers, 138–139

T
tables:
    bedside, *101*
    dining areas, 64–69
    kitchens, *83*, 86, 94
tableware:
    eating rooms, 69, 73, 76
    kitchens, *91*, 94
textures, 29, *30*
    bedrooms, *116*
towel rods, 124
towels, 126, 134

W
wet rooms, 131
window treatments, *23*
    bedrooms, *101*
    living rooms, 46
wish lists, 10–13
    bathrooms, 136–137
    bedrooms, 118–119
    eating rooms, 78–79
    kitchens, 96–97
    living rooms, 60–61
wow-factor, 58

Acknowledgements

A big thank you to Jan Baldwin, for her wonderful photographs, tireless patience, and being lots of fun.
Thanks to Fiona Lindsay of Limelight Management for believing in the book's concept, and to David Peters,
Alison Starling, and Gabriella Le Grazie, for giving it life. Thanks to Kate Brunt, for great locations, to
Catherine Randy, for a sophisticated design, and to Annabel Morgan, for her calm support and flawless editing.
Thank you to the owners of all the homes we visited, who cheerfully allowed not just their rooms, but the
contents of their closets, to be photographed. Thank you, Gabriele Sanders. Barely two months after
her partner, Timmy, was tragically killed during the New York September 11 2001 attack,
she still welcomed us into her home as a testament to the work they did on it together.
Thanks to Anthony, Cicely, and Felix, for being my favourite family. And to my parents, Harry and Ann,
who taught me that listmaking is the foundation of all great planning!